THE IMPORTANCE
OF MUSIC

BOOKS BY SIGMUND SPAETH

Milton's Knowledge of Music (Doctoral Dissertation)

The Common Sense of Music

Barber Shop Ballads (Foreword by Ring Lardner)

Words and Music

Read 'em and Weep: The Songs You Forgot to Remember

Weep Some More, my Lady

Listening

American Mountain Songs (with Ethel Park Richardson)

The Ampico in Music Study (with John Tasker Howard)

Gentlemen, Be Seated (with Dailey Paskman)

They Still Sing of Love

Music as a Social Force (with Gilbert Gabriel)

The Musical Adventures of Jack and Jill (Foreword by "Roxy")

The Home Song Book

The Art of Enjoying Music (also in Permabook edition)

The Facts of Life in Popular Song

Music for Everybody

Great Symphonies: How to Recognize and Remember Them

Great Program Music

Stories behind the World's Great Music

Maxims to Music (with Tony Sarg)

A Guide to Great Orchestral Music

Music for Fun

Opportunities in Music (Vocational Guidance Manual)

Fun with Music

55 Art Songs (with Carl O. Thompson)

At Home with Music

A History of Popular Music in America

Sigmund Spaeth's Song Session

Dedication: The Love Story of Clara and Robert Schumann

Fifty Years with Music (Foreword by Meredith Willson)

The Importance of Music (Foreword by Richard Rodgers)

THE IMPORTANCE
OF MUSIC

SIGMUND SPAETH

Foreword by Richard Rodgers

FLEET PUBLISHING CORPORATION

230 PARK AVENUE, NEW YORK 17, N.Y.

To
The Music Lovers of America

Foreword
By Richard Rodgers

Artists are given what is called "retrospective shows." The span of a life is spread out. The step by step growth of a man and his talent are displayed. Time, dates become focal. I would like to see a retrospective show of Sig Spaeth—his thirty-one books, and this, the thirty-second, his voluminous newspaper writings, his broadcasts and informal talks on music, his discoveries and his friendships, his vast influence in so many directions, all a part of a productive and purposeful life. Add to this the very important part he has played as a teacher of music in our generation.

A good teacher draws on many talents for his lessons. He uses precepts and examples. Humor, games, many other devices are a part of his skill. In all of these things, Sig's skill has been a high one.

I have often wondered about the many people, young and old, whom Sig has led into music. He knows Broadway like the village mailman. He has charted the growth of the musical theatre, its stumbling toward maturity, its groping for new expression. Who else knows Gershwin and Kern, Hindemith and barber shop ballads? For everything in music, Sig has been a Pied Piper of irresistible appeal. His appeal has been fun and enjoyment, and knowledge.

There's a point to be made for musical knowledge. It has been said that an appreciation of art cannot be obtained by aimlessly wandering in and out of art galleries. Music can be enjoyed casually—by an aimless exposure. But the enjoyment is greater when it is based on informed appreciation. The word I'd like to find falls somewhere between "sophistication" and "knowledge." Sig has been too young and enthusiastic in his pleasures to be called sophisticated, and too smart to try to impress anyone with the enormity of his knowledge.

In France, the title "Man of Letters" is an honor. It entitles you to sit way up at the head of the table.

A Man of Music should mean just as much.

Sig Spaeth is a Man of Music.

Preface

THE suggestion for this book came originally from Louis Biancolli, music editor of the New York *World-Telegram & Sun,* who felt that the author's *Fifty Years with Music* should be followed by a series of even shorter essays on various important aspects of music in general. The resulting material is largely based on syndicated columns appearing in local newspapers during the past few years, under the general title of "Music for Everybody," distributed and copyrighted by the General Features Corporation. The author has confined himself to topics presumably of interest to the layman (and possibly to the less complacent type of music-lover), eliminating, so far as possible, details of discussion which might have seemed too definitely dated.

The opinions expressed are purely personal, as they should be, and if they create violent disagreement, or even significant controversy, so much the better. At least they are completely honest, and unfortunately complete honesty still seems difficult to achieve in the complex field of music, with all its prejudices, exaggerated enthusiasms as well as criticisms, its frequently false values and its continued vulnerability to the ancient handicaps of snobbism and hypocrisy. There are still not enough people willing to face the facts concerning both serious and popular music, while too many self-nominated "experts" continue to hide a fundamental apathy under a coating of glib technicalities and facile echoes of artificial sentiments. There is ample and often sincere interest in star performers of all kinds, but the direct approach to music itself, for its own sake, is still a comparative rarity. If this little book stimulates such an approach in any actual or potential listeners, its publication will be amply justified.

The author is deeply grateful to Richard Rodgers for his kind contribution of a most friendly introduction. He also appreciates the opportunity of using the decorative sketches by Walt Trag and Henry Martin, made available by the magazine *Music Journal,* in which they first appeared. Such co-operation strengthens his already firm belief in the importance of music.

Sigmund Spaeth

January, 1963

Table of Contents

II. MORE TECHNICALLY SPEAKING

I

THE IMPORTANCE

OF MUSIC

Introductory

Isn't it about time that music was given the place it should rightfully have, not only among the arts but as one of the essentials of civilization? There has been a great deal of patronizing talk about the significance of music "from the cradle to the grave," its inspirational power in battle, its function as a mother's lullaby, etc. (Such generalizations are usually uttered by those most ignorant of its true possibilities.)

Actually music is as important to the human race as its literature and should be placed on the same level in our educational system. The eternal argument as to what is good or bad in both arts comes down eventually to a matter of personal opinion. But there are certain towering masterpieces of both literature and music whose permanent value is universally recognized. Below them lies a mass of material of varying appeal, subject to individual taste, and still lower is the garbage heap of unmitigated trash, unfortunately still the favorite haunt of the so-called "mass audience."

But concerning the exalted expressions of man's genius in music and literature there can be no disagreement. They have become established through the passage of time, not only by the careful study of conscientious scholars but by the cumulative approval of the average man himself.

It is on these heights that the choral works of Bach and Handel, the symphonies of Beethoven and Brahms, the operas of Mozart, Verdi and Wagner, and other musical masterpieces should share attention with the plays of Shakespeare and the poetry of Milton, Dante and Goethe, plus other works of recognized greatness. (Comparisons with contemporary creative art can easily be made in the teaching of such material.)

The chief reason for the neglect of music as a primary subject of education is that its technique is a complete mystery to the average person. People are constantly boasting that they "cannot read a note." It is generally assumed that some special talent is required for musical performance of any kind. (It helps, of course, but this is equally true of acting or public speaking, based upon a language which everybody knows to some extent.)

The fact that music represents a language that very few people can read or write unquestionably creates a handicap to the study of its literature. Yet it is the re-peated *hearing* of a masterpiece that counts, and the ability to read a score or write a musical theme is quite unnecessary. Actually the English of a school or college student is about as far from Shakespeare's as his attempts at musical expression would be from Beethoven.

This, then, is an urgent recommendation that music be treated in our educational institutions exactly as literature is treated. If there can be some study of its grammar and basic principles, so much the better. But before graduating from college (or even high school) every student should have been liberally exposed to the great masterpieces of music, with some consequent knowledge of their significance in civilization.

Far too much of a student's time is spent in the history of man's absurdities and imbecilities through the ages. Attention is wasted on a geography that changes daily through the whim of circumstance. Dead languages are studied laboriously, with the usual result of a smattering of etymology that might better have been acquired in a special course, while the classics of Greece and Rome were being enjoyed in the excellent translations available.

Physics and chemistry are presumably essential subjects in a scientific age, but their permanent usefulness is limited to those who make a career in engineering or the sciences. As for mathematics, the majority of those who struggle through the elaborate subjects following simple arithmetic (algebra, geometry, trigonometry, calculus, etc.) still find it difficult to keep a household account or make out an income tax declaration.

In such a curriculum music surely deserves a place of honor, instead of being treated as a stepchild. Apparently its chief sin is that one enjoys listening to it. But is there any law decreeing that the useful things in life must be unpleasant?

Which Is More Important?

IT is often said that a symphony is more important than an opera because its appeal depends entirely on the music itself, without any help from words, costumes, scenery and action. On the other hand, a "grand opera" is widely recognized as the most elaborate form of musical and dramatic composition, requiring the ability to write for voices as well as instruments and introducing such elements as ballet, pageantry and spectacle as needed, in addition to the inspired expression of basic human emotions.

It might well be argued that opera demands a versatility of talent in its creator and is actually an endless challenge to a composer's mastery of detail, making it perhaps the most difficult of all forms of art to bring to a successful completion. By comparison, a symphony may be considered far less complex, yet the very directness of its appeal creates problems perhaps just as challenging as those of the operatic stage.

Such a term as "absolute" or "pure" music applies most fittingly to a well-made symphony, for this type of composition, as a rule, gives the listener no hint of any definite meaning, depending for its effect on the combination of melodic inspiration, tonal design, instrumentation and the various details of creative technique and musicianship. If such a composition consistently affects its hearers in the same way, perhaps even with a suggestion of inevitability, it must command the highest respect as a work of art, for it has succeeded in expressing the abstract in concrete terms, which is the ideal of every sincere creative artist. To impart to practically every listener the abstract feeling of calm or excitement, courage or fear, dejection or triumph is an achievement indeed, and this has been accomplished to some extent by all the great masters of absolute music.

When a composer gives an instrumental piece a definite title, perhaps even adding more or less detailed explanatory notes to suggest the story or picture that is being tonally presented, the result is known technically as "program music," and this type of composition is generally regarded as more obvious and consequently less important than absolute music. There are, however, many works of musical significance regardless of any announced "program," and occasionally one finds even a symphony, like Beethoven's *Pastorale,* with definite indications of a pictorial or narrative quality.

When words are added to instrumental music, as in songs, choruses, cantatas, oratorios and operas, the "program" is of course made entirely clear, and this probably explains why vocal music is generally more popular than instrumental. If there is a definite text to tell a story, paint a picture or create a mood, the composer is naturally relieved of much of his burden of responsibility.

There are many songs in which the words are more important than the music, and it is by no means difficult to fit haphazard notes to a poem or even a piece of prose, merely following the natural accents, without bothering about melodic inspiration.

So the problems of musical composition still remain unsettled. Genius asserts itself in all forms, whether "absolute" or "programmatic," with or without a text; and the listener himself is the final judge of musical values.

Musical Megalomania

ONE of the questions constantly raised in the field of music is whether a composition in one of the larger forms, such as a symphony, a sonata, a concerto, a string quartet, an oratorio, cantata or opera, is necessarily more significant than a so-called "art song" or a comparatively short solo for the piano or some other individual instrument. The argument frequently suggests similar comparisons between a short story and a novel or play, a miniature and a life-sized painting, a chapel and a cathedral, a figurine and an heroic statue, or, in the world of Nature, a violet and an oak tree or a hummingbird and an eagle.

It is generally admitted that mere size should not be made a basis of comparison, in art or life in general. Certainly a good song has greater value than a bad symphony or opera. But when both works are of a high quality, perhaps even touched with genius, the problem becomes more difficult.

The mere fact that a large composition of any kind, in music, literature, painting, sculpture or architecture, demands more time and effort from its creator than does a comparatively small one must inevitably influence human reaction, and if such a *magnum opus* maintains a consistently high standard throughout, it may logically be considered superior to a miniature of any kind, no matter how perfect in its inspiration and technique. Actually, there are few gigantic works of art that sustain the highest level of creation throughout. There are almost sure to be unimpressive interludes, stopgaps, perhaps even some outright padding, connecting the obvious climaxes of pure inspiration, and the public generally accepts this alternation of the thrilling and the relatively prosaic without question.

There is always danger, however, of that megalomania which blindly glorifies size and length above all other aesthetic considerations. The crowds that invariably attend a performance of Beethoven's *Ninth Symphony* (or listen to it on records), are attracted largely by the fact that it adds a full chorus and four soloists to the orchestra. They may not even be aware that the choral Finale is actually less effective than the three purely instrumental movements. Many a rabid Wagnerite refuses to admit that the music-dramas of the Bayreuth master contain some dull passages that the composer himself would probably have deleted for modern audiences.

But one must guard also against the exaggerated ecstasy created by a practically perfect work of art of limited extent. It may defy improvement of any kind, but it is still a miniature as compared with a major achievement. Chopin, Schumann and Brahms all wrote short pieces for the piano that may be considered absolutely flawless. Yet one would hardly rank them above the same composers' concertos or sonatas. The German *Lied* and the French *Chanson* often represent perfection in the field of vocal music; but the best of these gems of inspiration cannot fairly be compared with a Bach cantata or mass, a Handel oratorio, or an opera by Mozart, Verdi or Wagner. Each example may be considered supreme in its field, but beyond this there is no basis for comparison.

Great composers invariably exhibit their genius in works of varying size and significance. Beethoven was not above arranging folk tunes or writing country dances and children's pieces. Bach was even more versatile in the gamut of his musical creations. Schubert produced songs and symphonies with equal facility. The true music-lover accepts all these treasures gratefully and appreciatively, without applying a yardstick or counting decibels.

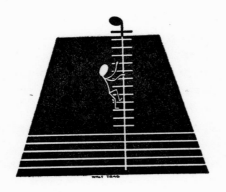

The "Goose Flesh" Response

THAT great violinist and human being, the late Fritz Kreisler, implied occasionally that a musical experience is worth while only if at some point one develops what is commonly known as "goose flesh." This phenomenon is difficult to describe, much less explain or analyze. People arrive at the sensation for a variety of reasons.

Often association, conscious or unconscious, has a great deal to do with it. A grown man will respond to a lullaby sung by his mother in his childhood, even if the music has comparatively little intrinsic value. A popular song of the past becomes temporarily a masterpiece because of its connection with some important occasion, like love at first sight, an engagement or a wedding.

Mere tradition may create a powerful and immediate response, as when college students sing their Alma Mater in victory or defeat. (Such tradition unquestionably had a real influence on the effect of an Indian medicine man's mumbo-jumbo and perhaps also the ancient Greek belief in the absolute "ethos" or ethical value attached to every type of scale or "mode," sometimes even the individual tones of such a scale.)

Regardless of any such background, the fact remains that throughout history millions of listeners have responded to the same music in approximately the same way. Thereby they have assured the permanence of a composition, which is accordingly listed as a "classic," or, in the popular field, a "standard." If such an emotional response becomes in time spontaneous and apparently inevitable, all argument automatically ceases. The piece is established as a favorite with the public. No amount of scholarly criticism or acclaim will make the slightest difference.

This universal emotional appeal is found in all kinds of music, from the intellectual technique of a Bach to the "Schmaltz" of a Grieg or a Tchaikovsky. It includes a great many folk tunes, such as our own river chantey "Shenandoah," Kentucky's "Lonesome Road" and some of the Negro spirituals.

The worst handicap of the serious contemporary composer is that he seldom gets enough hearings of any work to establish a dependable response on the part of his hearers. His music is unfamiliar to practically every audience, and, with a first performance too often the sum total of exposure to the public, he cannot logically expect any emotional effect of the type described by Mr. Kreisler.

There naturally follows the question whether such a response could ever be reasonably expected, regardless of the number of public hearings. There are many who frankly consider this a physical impossibility, claiming that modern music of the serious type is mostly cerebral, a product of the laboratory rather than a spontaneous expression of the heart. It is a complex and highly intellectual art. Its significance often depends upon details of technique of which the average listener is completely unaware.

One finds many gradations in modern musical expression, from mild dissonance to consistently ugly sounds, reaching a climax in the purely haphazard marking of tapes, with a final and absolute dismissal of the human equation. All of this may be interesting and even significant in the field of science. But will all our future music be scientific rather than inspired? And are we to renounce forever that unique experience of "goose flesh" which Fritz Kreisler recommended?

Musical Snobbery

A MUSIC critic who shall be nameless has gone on record, in print, with the statement that "we do not believe that the best music can or should be popularized." This is the frank admission of an attitude, shared also by some artists and teachers, which has definitely held back the honest enjoyment of good music in America by at least fifty years.

One hears considerable optimistic talk nowadays about the number of people who are buying records of the classics, attending concerts and opera performances, even playing various instruments in their homes. Unquestionably the number of such enthusiasts is greater than it has ever been in the past. The fact remains that well over ninety per cent of the American population is still comparatively untouched by the world's great music.

Executives of the record industry must admit that the big volume of sales will be found in the popular hits of the moment, mostly sung by teen-agers' idols. Adult taste, at best, runs mostly toward the albums of Broadway musicals of the day, actually representing a high standard in their own field. The all-time classics can be sold on a large scale only when interpreted by "big names" or offered at bargain prices through the various record clubs and libraries. The audience for contemporary music of a serious character is admittedly infinitesimal.

Much of this national backwardness in musical taste may be blamed on the insistence of our well-intentioned but narrow-minded scholars who have persisted in considering the potential audience for good music an automatically limited one.

Symphony orchestras, opera companies and concert courses are still too generally regarded as objects of charity, whose support is perhaps a duty but hardly an honest pleasure. The very word "culture" seems to create in the masses a curious suspicion bordering on contempt, and the "highbrow" or "egghead" is held up to ridicule.

Such a situation is not relieved by either snobbery or hypocrisy. The sincere music-lover must find ways of removing the mystery and the mumbo-jumbo from the world's great and permanent compositions in order to reach an enormous audience which is still virtually untouched. Without such an audience we can hardly expect the governmental support that will eventually prove an absolute necessity for the development of American music.

The Perils of Versatility

ONE of the chief distinctions between an amateur and a professional, particularly in the field of music, is that the former scatters his talents without ever becoming a real artist of any kind, whereas the latter finds out early what is the most promising activity and sticks to it until commercial success is attained.

The great geniuses of the world were practically all versatile, and could probably have made a living in any one of several arts and sciences. But they were wise enough to emphasize their most practical gifts and treat their additional abilities as hobbies.

The shining example is Michelangelo, supreme as a painter and sculptor, but also a poet, a musician and an engineer. His compatriot, Leonardo da Vinci, is best remembered by his paintings, but also had both literary and musical ability and as a scientist and inventor actually anticipated the possibilities of modern air travel. These two men were perhaps the most versatile geniuses of history. But even they could not afford to accept the traditional title of "Jack-of-all-trades."

It is now generally admitted that true genius may be expressed in various ways by the same individual. But the fact remains that a lasting reputation is usually gained in only one of several possible directions. Today the amateur who is clever at drawing or painting, playing an instrument, singing and composing, possibly also writing verse and prose, is by no means uncommon. But this very versatility defeats the chance for a professional career of any kind.

Felix Mendelssohn was amazingly gifted in practically all of the arts, and his life must be considered a success even though he is still ranked somewhat below the greatest composers of history. He was a spectacular pianist and an excellent conductor (the first to use a baton without actually playing in the orchestra). He wrote well, drew charming pictures and possessed all the social graces, with the advantage of a background of wealth and social position. (His father was a prominent banker and his grandfather a famous philosopher.)

With it all, Mendelssohn was a most lovable personality, happily married and with a host of friends. It seems almost cruel to suggest that he might have improved even on this remarkable record if he had concentrated on his music, particularly as a composer.

The great soprano, Marcella Sembrich, was undecided about her musical career, being equally gifted as a pianist, a violinist and a singer. It was her teacher and eventual husband, William Stengel, who made the decision for her, and she never regretted it. After an extraordinary career at the Metropolitan Opera she appeared in a gala farewell program, playing both a piano and a violin concerto and singing operatic arias and concert numbers.

Harold Bauer might have been a professional violinist, but wisely chose the piano as his instrument. Rachmaninoff was a concert pianist, an orchestral conductor and a composer, but he is remembered today chiefly for his creative work in music.

Leonard Bernstein is probably our most diversified contemporary artist, adding to his playing, conducting and composing an amazing ability as a writer, speaker and teacher via television. But he is concentrating more and more on the baton, and it is as a conductor that he will most likely be remembered. Professional musicians cannot afford to be too promiscuous with their talents.

Composer and Interpreter

THERE is still considerable argument over the comparative importance of the composer of a piece of music and its interpreter. In the popular field the arranger also appears prominently in the picture, and in that area the mere creator of a successful song is given the least credit of all.

Let it be admitted that a serious composition, such as a symphony or an opera, does not really come to life until it is performed by adequate interpreters. The notes written or printed on paper are no more than a guide for the players, singers and conductors who bring to the listeners a conception of what the composer had in mind and how he wanted his work to sound. The manuscript or published copy can offer only a certain number of directions, chiefly with regard to tempo and the most necessary gradations in volume, from loud to soft and vice versa.

There may be indications of "phrasing" by curved lines above the notes, plus the obvious rests and the grouping of measures. But in the long run the subtleties of interpretation are the responsibility of the performers rather than the creators of music.

Most of the sincere artists of concert and opera uphold the ideal of carrying out the intentions of the composer as meticulously as possible. "Tradition" is most important on the operatic stage, and singing actors are usually trained in a so-called "mise-en-scene" which demands rigid adherence to certain established positions, gestures and musical effects. Today, however, there is a trend toward originality of production, sometimes accepted and perhaps as often resented by the public.

(The outstanding examples of tampering with a composer's intentions are probably the current presentations of the Wagnerian music dramas at Bayreuth by Wagner's own grandsons, Wieland and Wolfgang, who insist, nevertheless, that they are doing exactly what their grandfather would have wished were he living today.)

Orchestral conductors generally have a feeling for tradition, and most of them have quite a clear idea of how a symphonic composer wanted his work to sound. The great Toscanini's reputation rested largely on the fact that he carried out a composer's intentions to the most minute detail. If these intentions were not absolutely clear, Toscanini nevertheless created that impression by his interpretations.

Actually, it is always a temptation to the conductor of a symphony orchestra to impose his own ideas upon the work that is being performed, and there have been cases of a "prima donna complex" which made the audience far more aware of the man on the podium than of the creator of the composition. In extreme instances this has resulted literally in a desecration of great music.

No such independence of interpretation, however, can possibly compare with the constant distortion of the creations of our popular composers. Here the arrangers are partly to blame, and in fairness it should be confessed that a skillful arrangement has often contributed significantly to the making of a hit song. But the liberties taken by our "song stylists" with the melody, the rhythm and even the words of a popular song are generally inexcusable.

As if it were not enough to ignore the names of the creators of our popular music, these "interpreters" do everything they can to insult their intelligence, as well as that of their listeners. It may not matter particularly so far as the average output of Tin Pan Alley is concerned, but a Gershwin, a Kern, a Rodgers, a Berlin or a Porter should be given credit for knowing his business.

Are these "song stylists" unable to read notes? Or do they realize that singing a song as it is written would put them into hopeless competition with really good voices?

The Effect of Inevitability

THE technique of music can be studied, in theory and in practice, and almost anyone can acquire some appreciation of the subtleties of rhythm, melody, harmony, tone color and form. Fortunately even this basic knowledge is not strictly necessary for the honest enjoyment of some type of music, and an adequate taste may be developed by the mere process of being exposed to compositions of all kinds. But "inspiration" still remains an almost insoluble riddle.

Why should a certain progression of tones produce an emotional thrill, perhaps even a definite feeling of excitement, exaltation or sadness, when the same tones in a different order or rhythmic pattern have no effect whatever on the average listener? The impression of inevitability actually enters into human reactions to so-called "melodic inspiration" and this again is impossible to explain or analyze.

The word "inspire" means literally "to breathe into,"

and the related noun "spirit," from the same Latin root, implies the breath of life, a mysterious reality not of this world, something apart from the physical or even the mental, in short what is generally called "the soul." To the artist in general, as well as to primitive man, there is no difficulty in believing in the direct communication of a mysterious instinct, often called a "divine afflatus," which results in the phenomenon ultimately recognized as inspiration. Composers like Handel, Haydn and Beethoven never hesitated to credit their successful creations to the divine influence of God Himself, and this belief has been shared by many an artist of less pronounced religious faith. The mystery remains, regardless of any explanation.

Assuming that the great inspirations of music and art in general can properly be considered expressions of true Divinity, how is one to regard the countless "inevitabilities" of minor significance? Can one apply the word "inspiration" to a perfect folk song, a Strauss waltz, a Foster melody, even a popular hit which has proved its permanence?

It may perhaps be fairly claimed that any work of art that definitely carries out the intention of its creator and transfers that ideal to the unprejudiced observer has a right to be called "inspired." Such an effect is obviously easier to achieve on a small scale than in a work of substantial proportions. It is often said that at certain points in an opera, an oratorio or a symphony the composer's "inspiration flagged." This may not seriously affect the appeal of the work as a whole. In fact, it would be difficult to name any substantial musical composition that can honestly be considered inspired from start to finish.

The important point is still the common reaction of millions to what impresses them, perhaps subconsciously, as inevitable. If a composer intends merely to write an effective song, or a little piano piece, and accomplishes this to the complete satisfaction of the listener, he should not be deprived of the credit for inspiration even if his achievement is on a very modest scale. If he has produced what he intended and the result is consistently recognized as exactly "right," there need be no argument as to just how this was accomplished.

Temper and Temperament

THE word "temperament" is frequently applied to musicians of all kinds, but there have been few attempts to explain the term, most of them unsuccessful. Actually the public is almost always aware of its presence in an artist but equally powerless in arriving at any satisfactory definition or analysis.

To some people "temperament" means practically the same thing as "temper," and they are more interested in its manifestations off-stage than as part of a performer's equipment. Whatever its psychological basis may be, the fact remains that real temperament inevitably conveys itself to an audience and at its best must be considered a sincere and instinctive expression of personality.

Mannerisms and affectations have little or nothing to do with the matter, although they are sometimes developed deliberately in a desperate attempt to suggest a temperament that is actually lacking. Again the public usually succeeds in separating the false from the true.

When real temperament asserts itself, there is no doubt whatever as to its fascinating effect.

There is a general feeling that European musicians are more temperamental than Americans, and this may be closer to the truth than some of us are willing to admit. In general our artists are inclined to be almost matter-of-fact in their straightforwardness. They find it difficult, if not impossible, to assume an artificial personality, preferring to let their art speak for itself. Yet it should be remembered that perhaps the most notorious "prima donna" of our time, Maria Callas, is American-born, although of Greek parentage.

According to legend and actual history, the temperamental outbursts of the past, particularly among singers, were almost incredible and would certainly not be tolerated today. They were mostly the result of an enormous vanity, which is still a prime necessity for any successful performer, for without such supreme self-confidence a critical public could never be faced. (It might be added parenthetically that the most obviously conceited artists have generally been those who were not entirely sure of themselves, perhaps even secretly troubled by an inferiority complex. The truly great men and women of music have consistently created the impression of a sincere humility, even when they were quite obviously aware of the significance of their tremendous gifts.)

Among the famous temperaments of history were those of Francesca Cuzzoni and Faustina Bordoni, whose rivalry drove the composer Handel to distraction. (He once threatened the former with physical violence in the course of a heated argument.) Caterina Gabrielli appar-

ently showed her temperament chiefly by flirting with
forbidden gentlemen such as Count Potemkin, the favorite of Catherine the Great, who naturally resented this
intrusion. Such stars as Maria Malibran, Henrietta Sonn-
tag, even Adelina Patti and Nellie Melba, were immortalized in spectacular tales of their temperamental outbursts
as well as by their slavish devotion to art.

Composers have often shared the spotlight of temperament with musical performers, the fabulous Franz Liszt
making an almost unique reputation in both fields. Beethoven was noted for his boorish ways and complete independence of social convention, even in relations with his
noble patrons. Haydn, on the other hand, accepted life
with complacent equanimity, always thanking God for
his creative inspirations.

The great Bach was similar in his religious humility
and essentially a modest man, who looked upon music
chiefly as a job to be performed to the best of his ability.
Brahms also showed few signs of temperament, although
he could be decidedly rude to disguise his essential shy-
ness. Wagner, on the other hand, possessed a flamboyant
personality that consistently ignored common courtesy.

One of the most modest composers of all time was Robert Schumann, yet he eventually attempted suicide and
died in a mental institution at the age of forty-six. Both
Mozart and Schubert, famous for their sunny dispositions
and easy-going manner of life, died in their thirties, while
Mendelssohn, perhaps the most untemperamental of composers, also failed to reach his fortieth year, as did the
contrastingly mercurial Chopin.

Apparently temperament has little to do with longevity or, for that matter, personal popularity. But its effect on the success of an artist can hardly be denied.

Visualizing
Musical Performance

THERE are still many people who think that music should be seen as well as heard. They are the ones who tempt good artists to add exaggerated and artificial gestures to their performances, refusing to let the music speak for itself and emphasizing the obvious with a variety of mannerisms.

A pianist is expected to bend down close to the keyboard when playing very softly and, vice versa, to bring his hands down from above his head to signal the approach of a crashing chord. A rapid scale passage must end with the fingers apparently flying into outer space, as though the piano did not offer enough keys to contain the infinite progression.

Similarly violinists are encouraged to sway with closed eyes and a beatific facial expression while interpreting a ravishing melody, to dig their chins into their instruments and lean forward during fast examples of technique and to lift the bow toward the stars as a signal that such difficult problems have been successfully solved.

The dramatic gestures of an orchestral conductor have almost limitless possibilities. The big sweep of the arms, to indicate *fortissimo,* the sudden drop to a low level for a contrasting *pianissimo,* perhaps emphasized by a finger on the lips, the trembling of the entire body to express passionate ecstasy—these are mere starting points for making an orchestral performance visible as well as audible.

How much of these eye-filling dramatizations may be considered natural, sincere and spontaneous, and how much could be put down to deliberate acting—this is an open question and likely to remain so. Admittedly there are musicians of all kinds who almost instinctively express their emotions in more ways than by the combination of tone and technique. Leonard Bernstein apparently cannot help moving his body in time to an exciting rhythm or letting his face assume a rapturous expression while conducting an honestly moving melody, discarding a few more inhibitions when on television.

Leopold Stokowski, generally considered the master showman of the baton, may be sincere in many of the dramatic details of his orchestral performances, and the brilliance of his musicianship remains undisputed even when his interpretation of a masterpiece becomes an acting tour de force as well as an exciting musical experience. On the other hand, conductors like Fritz Reiner and Pierre Monteux consistently succeed in producing effects of sublime beauty with a minimum of physical activity and a notable economy of gesture.

That great violinist, Jascha Heifetz, has often been accused of coldness because he refused to dramatize in action the music he played so perfectly. Fritz Kreisler was also impersonal in his attitude toward a composition, substituting sincerity and a warmth of tone for possible acrobatics on the concert stage. Mischa Elman, however, still the possessor of great tonal beauty and technical command of the violin, has never lost the youthful habit of conveying his emotion through facial and bodily expression as well as musically.

Rudolf Serkin, once a very staid and apparently unemotional pianist, has gradually developed certain mannerisms which unquestionably please his listeners and may actually represent a normal *crescendo* in style. Artur Rubinstein has never suffered from inhibitions at the keyboard and seems quite willing to act out a piece while making it sound absolutely fascinating. The extreme of such visual performance is probably represented by the popular young pianist Glenn Gould, who turns everything he plays into melodrama, to the obvious delight of every audience.

Don't blame the artists if they seem to overact at times. The people who pay to hear them love their music that way.

Concerning Musical Taste

Just how good is our taste in music? Certainly the number of those who honestly enjoy the established masterpieces is a limited one, representing perhaps less than one per cent of the population. There are even fewer who manifest a sincere interest in contemporary composition, although their ranks are swelled by various hypocrites and snobs who are secretly bored to death with the modern idiom.

Even the solid music lovers are often surprisingly ignorant of the details of symphonic structure, the difference between folk and art song, program and absolute music, etc. At least they have heard enough good music to acquire a fairly dependable taste, supported by their convictions and a willingness to express them. Rarest of all is the person sufficiently confident and well enough equipped to express a definite opinion at the first hearing of an unfamiliar work, regardless of the verdict of posterity.

This applies even to professional musicians, as well as critics and musical scholars.

The majority of the American public, so far as they listen to music at all, are content with the light classics and popular tunes associated with their own lives. There is a fairly large audience for jazz of various types, and some of the experts are just as vociferous and snobbish in expressing their tastes as the most high-brow of the long-hairs. To the bottom layer of Rock 'n' Roll fans there need not be attributed any musical authority whatever, as they are mostly too young to know any better.

Between this rock bottom of ignorance and the exalted, perhaps ultra-precious tastes of a handful of connoisseurs, there are millions who take their music in a perpetual state of comfortable coma or luscious lethargy. They use it mostly as a background for whatever they may be doing, and this habit is recognized by the record manufacturers, who now give their albums of mood music descriptive titles to fit almost any situation. There are even discs guaranteed to put people to sleep, and unquestionably a great deal of music is heard while reading, eating, conversing or doing housework.

The High Priests of such music are conductors like Lawrence Welk and Mantovani. Much of the background music of motion pictures is of the same type, and we hear it also piped into restaurants and industrial plants by the Muzak system or some similar vending machine. (The jukebox is on a somewhat lower level, giving still greater encouragement to a taste for the obvious.)

There is nothing radically wrong about this basically sensuous approach to music, even though it clearly represents the line of least resistance. No one could expect an entire population to develop suddenly into music students. But may it not be possible for us gradually to respond to music somewhat as we respond to sports, acquiring at least the minimum information as to what it is all about?

Nationalistic Music

NATIONALISM, long a menace to civilization, has affected the world's music as well, often with strange results. It may be claimed in general that the great music of all time is, on the whole, free from national characteristics, whereas the works exhibiting a strong nationalism are generally written by composers of lesser significance.

It is also probably true that obviously nationalistic music is likely to exert a more immediate appeal than compositions of a more cosmopolitan nature, failing, however, in most cases, to establish a reputation as a work of enduring value in the judgment of connoisseurs. Music of a marked national flavor arrives fairly easily at a quick popularity, but rarely succeeds in achieving the status of the more complex masterpieces.

An outstanding example is found in the works of the Norwegian composer, Edvard Grieg. There is no mistaking their nationality or their instantaneous effect. Yet their creator remains a comparatively minor figure in the history of the world's music, unable to compete on equal terms with the giants who developed profounder and more universal forms of expression.

The most strongly nationalistic music of our time is unquestionably that of Spain, a country which has also preserved its distinctive folk music right up to the present. Yet there are practically no Spanish composers of world-wide reputation, and literally none to compare with the recognized creative geniuses. Isaac Albeniz, Manuel de Falla and Enrique Granados are about the only names that would occur even to a devotee of musical composition as representatives of Spain. All three wrote effective pieces of markedly national character, but not one of them can be credited with a true masterpiece in a larger form. Curiously enough, some of the most popular Spanish music was written by the French composers Bizet, Chabrier and Lalo and Russia's Rimsky-Korsakoff, but they all borrowed somewhat from actual melodies of Spain. (Bizet's famous "Habanera" in *Carmen* was originally composed by Sebastian Yradier.)

Franz Liszt attained a Hungarian flavor only in the Rhapsodies based on the folk tunes of his native land, and these are deservedly his most popular compositions. His larger works might equally well have been written by a composer of any nationality. On the other hand, Bela Bartok, while strongly influenced by Hungarian folk music, was not enslaved by nationalism but attained a true universality of expression in contemporary terms.

Moussorgsky was unquestionably the most nationalistic of Russian composers and may in time prove the exception to the rule. But it is Tchaikovsky who is generally classed with the great symphonists, and his music, except for the occasional use of a folk tune, might equally well have been written by a German. Rimsky's versatility enabled him to interpret almost any kind of folk music, including the Russian. Stravinsky's early compositions, particularly *Petrouchka,* possessed a Russian flavor, but he later abandoned nationalism, as did Prokofiev and Shostakovitch.

It would be wrong to label the greatest music of Germany, France and Italy as "nationalistic," for it goes far beyond such boundaries even when it shows a distinctive and unmistakable style. On the other hand, Chopin's most popular compositions have a definitely Polish quality, largely due to his incorporation of national rhythms such as the Mazurka and the Polonaise.

Coming finally to the United States of America, it should be admitted frankly that our most characteristic music is in the popular field, and particularly in the jazz idiom. Of our more serious creative musicians only George Gershwin attained a truly American style, and he was essentially a popular composer. Ironically enough, the most characteristically American symphony was written by the Bohemian composer Anton Dvorak, entitled *From the New World.* Composers in general do best when they disregard nationalism in favor of humanity and the beauty of universally recognized truth.

The Teaching of Music

THE voice of the music teacher is being heard throughout the land. Thousands of educators all over America are initiating their pupils into the mysteries of the piano, the violin and other instruments, with even more concentrating on the training of the human voice.

Many of these teachers are progressive and practical in their methods, adapting themselves to the possibilities and limitations of their charges, satisfied if they produce results that may be considered logical. But there are still some pedagogues of the old-fashioned kind who follow a routine set of rules and formulas, treating every student in approximately the same fashion, with little regard for differences of character, environment, personality and even innate ability.

Perhaps the greatest mistake made by our music teachers of the past (including a few of the present) has been to overemphasize the importance of technique as such. (This of course applies to the study of musical instruments rather than to the development of the singing voice, although even here there has been a tendency to respect vocal fireworks in preference to a natural beauty of tone and a solid musicianship.)

It would be absurd to argue that anyone can become a performing artist without some degree of technical skill, and this applies to the serious amateur as well as to the actual or potential professional, to whom a brilliant technique is absolutely essential and usually taken for granted. It may be claimed that every music student of more than average ability should be encouraged (perhaps even compelled) to practice at least enough to insure the adequate command of whatever compositions may fit into a balanced repertoire. Unfortunately, native ability and industry are not always found in the same individual.

But why, after all, should a music teacher's market be limited to those possessing an obvious talent? Under such restrictions, musical instruction is automatically restricted to a very small percentage of the public. Why should the great majority of people, adults as well as children, be ignored completely in our efforts toward a more general participation in music? This makes no sense either culturally or commercially.

One still hears of those who "took" for so many years and "don't know a single piece today." Generally the answer is that they were kept at the drudgery of scales and exercises, instead of being allowed to play music requiring practically no technique, of which there is a vast literature available. Just what did the old-fashioned teacher think was accomplished by all this dull routine? Most of these pupils would never play well in any case, but they might at least have been developing an honest love of music and the satisfaction of a modest self-expression instead of being completely bored. Incidentally, the same amount of effort applied to the keys of a typewriter rather than a piano would have produced far more practical results.

Our music teachers are still overlooking an enormous number of possible pupils because of this firmly grounded tradition of potential artistry. There are housewives and businessmen who would enjoy playing a musical instrument for their own pleasure, without any thought of showing off or astonishing the neighbors. They have no time for intensive practice, but could make satisfactory progress within the lesson periods themselves. Often they could work in groups, with individual attention provided whenever justified by unsuspected ability or honest enthusiasm.

Look around you, music teachers. There is real work still to be done.

What Price Chamber Music?

CHAMBER music enjoys the distinction of being the form most respected by connoisseurs and least appreciated by the general public. There was a time when stock musical jokes included a description of a chamber music concert as one in which "the players come in one by one and the audience goes out the same way."

Yet in those days, one could hear several string quartets of the highest rank, including the famous Kneisel Quartet, headed by the concertmaster of the Boston Symphony Orchestra, and the Flonzaley Quartet, representing the French style of playing, originally subsidized by a wealthy music-lover named DeCoppet. There was also the Olive Mead Quartet, composed entirely of feminine performers. Hans Letz, at one time a member of the Kneisel group, later organized his own quartet, and some of today's music-lovers may remember the Kolisch Quartet, headed by a left-handed violinist, Rudolf Kolisch. (This oddity was considered an advantage because it permitted both the first and second violins to be turned toward the audience while their players faced each other.)

Of late, there seems to be a rather disturbing decrease in the public performance of chamber music. One is forced to believe that many self-styled music-lovers of today are not even quite sure of the exact meaning of the term "chamber music." All they know is that it supposedly appeals to the intellect rather than to the emotions and cannot be played in a hall large enough to make it pay (although this has often been done, with generally unfortunate artistic results).

Obviously the word "chamber" implies the use of a comparatively small room, and this is literally necessary for chamber music at its best. The Germans called it *Kammermusik* and traced it back to the days when almost all music performed outside of the church was presented under the patronage of royalty or nobility and of necessity in rather intimate surroundings. Originally such performances included vocal as well as instrumental music, but today chamber music is technically limited to small groups of instruments, presumably of equal individual significance. (A violinist accompanied by the piano is considered a recitalist, but if the two are performing sonatas, on a basis of equality, it is regarded as chamber music.)

The commonest and most popular chamber ensemble is the string quartet, and this group may be increased to a quintet, sextet, etc., by the addition of other instruments, including the piano, or the doubling of certain parts. There is also the classic "trio," consisting of violin, cello and piano, unfortunately now associated too often with summer hotels.

While the public performance of chamber music is unquestionably decreasing, there is an encouraging interest in the informal interpretation of this highly specialized music, particularly in our colleges and universities, many of which boast professional string quartets in residence in addition to groups of students and faculty members who play chiefly for their own pleasure. Today there is emphasis also on various combinations of wind instruments, always pleasing to listeners as well as performers, and of course we still have with us the inevitable jazz "combos," which might be termed "popular" chamber music, often representing a high degree of skill.

Finally, there is that valuable organization known as the Amateur Chamber Music Players, whose large membership list makes it possible for any enthusiast to find congenial players of approximately the same ability wherever he or she may happen to be, so that impromptu sessions of chamber music can be arranged almost anywhere on short notice. This is really the ideal of chamber music —to gratify its interpreters rather than listeners of perhaps doubtful comprehension. Under such conditions the art of chamber music can never really die.

Know Your Operas

IF you really want to enjoy a grand opera, regardless of the language in which it is sung, it will pay you to read the libretto in advance, or at least to skim through a fairly complete summary of the plot. This applies to opera in English as well as to opera in a foreign tongue.

There are several reasons for the audience's inability to understand the greater part of the text of any elaborate and serious operatic production. The bad enunciation of singers who concentrate on tonal quality rather than intelligibility is only a part of the story. Admittedly the cast of the average grand opera cannot compare with that of a Broadway musical in making the words absolutely clear to the listener. But this is not entirely their fault.

Much depends on the orchestration, the vocal range, the tempo, the style of the language and other details. Whenever even two voices are singing different words together, clarity of enunciation becomes almost impossible. As more voices are added, the obscurity increases, and often a large chorus might just as well be singing nonsense syllables for all that an audience can grasp of their words. (This applies to some extent also to choral performances on the concert stage.)

Perhaps the listeners, too, are partly to blame. They are so hypnotized by the effect of beautiful tones and so fascinated by details of action, costumes and scenery in the opera house that they fail to exercise the concentration essential to the understanding of the text. The fact remains that their supposed familiarity with even the English language is of little help.

A skilled composer knows how to bring out the really important words, often permitting a phrase to be sung without accompaniment of any kind, and in such cases the meaning is of course inescapable. He can adapt his harmony and instrumentation to the needs of the text, emphasizing certain passages and allowing others to be submerged in a flood of tonal beauty.

In the lighter field, Gilbert and Sullivan were masters of this technique. Their patter songs had a mere skeleton accompaniment, while a sentimental melody was given full play, without too much concern for verbal details. This system has been followed by most successful writers of musical comedy, with additional help from their interpreters.

The current tendency among American composers of serious opera is to select materials that do not lend themselves easily to the simple, dramatic treatment demanded by this art form. Their dialogue is often too complicated, with too many characters singing across and against each other, with predictably confusing results.

This brings us back to the original contention that the full enjoyment of a grand opera can be attained only through some preliminary homework. In listening to an operatic broadcast, it is advisable to follow every line with a libretto, an advantage which is impossible in the actual opera house. Let there be no self-deception as to the intelligibility of the text, regardless of the language concerned.

America's Serious Music

THERE has been much discussion of American music and also considerable action on the part of those who are sincerely interested in its promotion. On the other hand, an enthusiastic lip service has not always been turned into practical action. On the whole, the American composer of serious music still languishes in a state of neglect, public indifference, and often a faintly disguised hostility.

In general it may fairly be stated that our music critics despise most of the earlier American works, while our audiences are bored by the contemporary repertoire. This naturally creates an impasse which is difficult to overcome.

The situation is further complicated by a widespread hypocrisy, which affects not only the listeners but occasionally the scholars as well, and perhaps even the interpreters of American music. It is easier to get on the bandwagon and pretend a rapturous response than to voice an individual objection, and since many works never get past a first performance, at least for the ears of an individual hearer, a fair and judicious appraisal is practically impossible.

Another handicap lies in the fact that a great number of amateur composers manage to secure a hearing somehow, and the obvious shortcomings of their creations may easily persuade the average listener that all American music is equally bad. Add to the confusion the tub-thumping of hired press agents, the logrolling of generous-minded colleagues (balanced by attacks from jealous rivals), the inevitably optimistic advertisements and the vapid comments of well-intentioned but musically ignorant chauvinists, and you are faced with quite a problem.

Richard Korn, a conductor of international reputation, has presented a number of orchestral concerts in Carnegie Hall entirely devoted to America's composers, particularly those of the past. They were venomously treated by some of the critics, although the audiences showed consistent enthusiasm. Apparently "museum pieces" are frowned upon by experts, but enjoyed by the unsophisticated concert-goer.

The National Association for American Composers and Conductors, founded by Henry Hadley, proposes the establishment of a library of recordings covering the entire history of serious musical composition in the United States, a project which should appeal to the Ford Foundation, which has already performed such signal services to American music. Regardless of criticism and some natural reservations, it is generally agreed that America's musical creations must be heard not once but many times to arrive at a sincere appraisal and an honest appreciation. A "first performance" means little or nothing. The fifth, tenth and twentieth are the ones that count.

"American" Composers?

UNQUESTIONABLY, an enormous amount of music is being created by composers either born in this country or adopted by it. A fairly substantial percentage of this output arrives at public performance of some kind, regardless of its worth. To what extent the public is able to appraise its value is another question. So also is the problem of nationality as applied to foreign-born musicians, whether naturalized American citizens or not. It is gratifying to claim such renowned figures as Stravinsky, Hindemith, Krenek, Bloch and Menotti as our own, but to what extent can they be considered truly "American"?

This brings up another problem. In what ways can any of our contemporary music be recognized as typically American, and to what extent is such a characterization really necessary? Our earlier compositions were actually well-made imitations of European music, and this is still true of a considerable amount of material optimistically labelled "American."

Is it necessary to use folk themes to establish an American atmosphere? If so, how many of these basic melodies can themselves be claimed by this country, since so much of this music was thrown into the melting-pot by immigrants from various European localities?

In the long run, it may be simplest and most practical to call any music written by a composer living in the United States "American," leaving it to the critics and connoisseurs to compare it with the current European product. If any recognizably American characteristics can be found in it, so much the better. Most important, however, is the fact that it must be good music, able to hold its own in competition with other works of the present and even the past.

Here is the fundamental difficulty in the appraisal of American compositions. Our audiences have grown so accustomed to the acknowledged beauties of the world's musical masterpieces that they hesitate to recognize the possible value of less familiar material. Actually, they can hardly be expected to grasp such values at a single hearing, and unfortunately that is all they are likely to get in most cases.

Moreover, their taste has been largely formed not only by repeated performances of the recognized classics but also by the obvious fact that these works represent the survival of the fittest, the cream of the output of the great musical geniuses of all time. It is manifestly unfair to compare American music always with the best products of the past, representing all the rest of the world. Some excellent foreign composers could hardly survive such a test.

Perhaps the answer to the entire problem lies in a greater number of performances of a smaller total of compositions. Our leading creators of serious music do not have much difficulty in getting a hearing and sometimes several.

But who is to decide what is worthy of a first hearing, much less the repeated performances essential to public recognition? Our orchestral conductors and individual soloists are fairly conscientious in their search for new material that has a chance of acceptance. But various influences are constantly at work, sometimes in support of outright amateurs, and, after our long-suffering listeners have met with one disappointment after another, they are likely to lose confidence both in their own judgment and in the intrinsic possibilities of American music in general. One can only wait patiently and hope that somehow permanent values will eventually be discovered by the public, which is always the final judge.

American Musicians in General

In the early days of America's so-called "musical life," the accent was entirely on foreign products, creative as well as interpretive. Our composers wrote conventional imitations of European music, and our singers and instrumentalists had to study abroad, buy their first notices there and often actually Italianize their names to command attention at home.

Our supporters of concerts and the opera were, to a large extent, hypocritical in pretending an enthusiasm for good music which was entirely beyond their conception. The mania for foreign labels was naturally encouraged and to some extent created by European performers and teachers who came to the United States to tell us what musical barbarians we were and to pocket fat fees for their supposed superiority.

It has been the case that, with a few striking exceptions, American artists who have achieved success in important competitions abroad have been largely ignored in their own country while we continued to glorify the foreign musicians.

Presumably, conditions today are improved; however the tradition actually lingers on, and American-born creators and interpreters of music still have to be considerably better than their European competitors to hold their own.

American musicians generally find it difficult to simulate temperament or develop mannerisms of the kind that the public apparently loves. They are mostly straightforward, practical people, who regard music as a logical source of income for those who are properly equipped for commercial as well as artistic success.

They do not make newspaper headlines with spectacular escapades or controversial pronouncements. They behave like decent, normal citizens and deliver honest musical values to those who pay for tickets to hear them. But this does not seem to be enough when pitted against the sensational personalities of European "stars" whose ability is generally taken for granted.

The American composer is not doing badly these days, securing performances which may not always be merited. But our conductors are too often pushed aside in favor of comparatively unknown foreigners. Chauvinism has no place in music, but one cannot help wishing for a merit system that would concentrate on musical values, regardless of nationality.

The Music of Wagner

MORE and more one arrives at the conviction that the true glory of Richard Wagner lies in his music and nothing else. He has ignored most of the axioms of good theatre, and his philosophy is a childishly muddled affair.

Even his gods and goddesses become very ordinary human beings in their jealousies, their frustrations, their stupid plots and their selfish schemings for power. But over every insult to dramatic tradition, every unsingable phrase, every verbose puzzle of alliteration in the tiresomely repetitive text, the orchestral music soars triumphantly, the unforgettable inspiration of pure genius.

The four dramas of the Ring cycle have actually been compared with a gigantic symphony, each representing one movement, with *Siegfried* the Scherzo and *Götterdämmerung* the Finale. But each of these movements has within itself the material for at least half a dozen great symphonies of different types. Some purely orchestral passages, like the "Forest Murmurs" and the "Rhine Journey," have been frequently played in the concert hall, and there are others that can be performed with similar effect by the addition of one or two voices, or by embodying the vocal parts in the instrumental score.

Unquestionably, Wagner himself would have insisted upon drastic cuts in his music dramas if he were alive today, especially if he were thinking in terms of American audiences. The "perfect Wagnerite" naturally refuses to omit a single note, and at Bayreuth they solve the problem by giving the listeners time for full meals between acts and making a single production practically a day's work.

Actually all four of the Ring dramas could be held down to the length of *Das Rheingold* (two and a half hours) without harming the plot or the action. But to kill so much great orchestral music would be tragic.

Shakespeare in Music

WILLIAM SHAKESPEARE had a far greater effect on music than is generally realized.

Most people will be surprised to know that more than seventy-five operas have been based on Shakespeare's plays, and even confirmed music lovers may not be aware of many beyond Verdi's *Otello, Falstaff* and *Macbeth,* Nicolai's *Merry Wives of Windsor,* Gounod's *Romeo and Juliet* and perhaps the current *Taming of the Shrew* by Vittorio Giannini and Cole Porter's *Kiss Me, Kate,* with the same background via the Spewacks, Bella and Sam.

How many opera fans are aware that *Romeo and Juliet* has had no less than ten settings (not counting Tchaikovsky's Overture and Duet or the Berlioz Symphony), *The Merry Wives of Windsor* nine, *A Midsummer Night's Dream* eight (plus the famous Overture and Incidental Music of Mendelssohn), *The Tempest* seven and *Hamlet, Macbeth* and *The Merchant of Venice* six each?

Handel's *Julius Caesar* and Rossini's *Otello* have been

heard recently in concert form, and there is occasional mention (but no performance) of the Thomas *Hamlet,* the Bloch *Macbeth* and Wagner's *Liebesverbot,* based on *Measure for Measure.*

But who ever heard of Frazzi's *King Lear,* Eggen's *Cymbeline,* Salvayre's *Richard III,* Malipiero's *Anthony and Cleopatra* or Goldmark's *A Winter's Tale?* Edward German's dances for *Henry VIII* are often played, but the Saint-Saëns version of the entire drama remains a mystery.

It is perhaps worth noting that Shakespeare is gradually finding his way to the Broadway musical stage, as the hugely successful *Kiss Me, Kate* (*Taming of the Shrew*) is now joined by *West Side Story,* a modernization of the Romeo and Juliet story. There are nostalgic memories also of the Rodgers and Hart *Boys from Syracuse,* which had *The Comedy of Errors* as a background.

Aside from a fairly large body of instrumental music inspired by Shakespeare (with *Romeo and Juliet, Hamlet* and *A Midsummer Night's Dream* in the lead), there are of course the immortal songs for which the great dramatist supplied exceedingly singable lyrics. The best known are probably Franz Schubert's settings of "Who Is Sylvia?" and "Hark, Hark, the Lark," (the melody of which was composed on the back of a bill of fare).

But many other Shakespearean texts are still frequently heard, with music by such composers as Henry Purcell, Thomas Arne, Henry Carey and Sir Henry Bishop. Among the most popular examples are "Under the Greenwood Tree," "It Was a Lover and His Lass," "Come unto These Yellow Sands," and "Blow, Blow, Thou Winter Wind."

Shakespeare was unquestionably a practical musician as well as a playwright, aware of the dramatic value of music, especially the contrast and comic relief often provided by a lighthearted song. He was one of only three poets who really knew much about music. (The others were John Milton and Robert Browning, the first a gifted organist and singer, the second a scholar and analyst, with a command of technical terms, but faulty judgment.)

There is no other figure in literature who affected the history and materials of music as did William Shakespeare.

Music and Painting

THE great painters of the world have often selected musical subjects for their pictures. Some of these have become justly famous. Picasso's *Three Musicians,* for instance, is one of the most popular of the works on exhibition at New York's Museum of Modern Art.

Of this fascinating painting, created in 1921, Alfred H. Barr, Jr. in *Masters of Modern Art* writes: "It is not only one of Picasso's climactic achievements, it is perhaps the culminating work of cubism." He describes the three musicians as representing the old commedia dell' arte figures. Pierrot, in white, plays a recorder; Harlequin is in the center with a guitar; and at the right is a strange apparition, apparently singing behind his veiled mask. According to Mr. Barr, Picasso "transforms the three music-making comedians into a solemn and majestic triumvirate."

In contrast to this modern masterpiece is a gem of the sixteenth century called *Three Musical Ladies,* whose

Flemish painter is known only as "The Master of the Half Lengths." Here everything is clear and simple, with the lute-playing, singing ladies obviously snatching a few moments of peace during the period of almost continuous war.

One of the best known of all musical pictures is *The Jester,* by the Dutch Frans Hals; often called *The Lute-Player,* it is full of life and color, suggesting actual sound. Again a contrast is offered by the modern Manet's *The Fifer,* a perky little boy in red trousers and a fancy cap, familiar to all who have visited the Louvre.

The Italian Carpaccio painted a famous *Angel with Lute,* like Peter Pan sitting cross-legged in front of a window. And there is a feminine *Lute Player* by da Caravaggio, as well as a *Girl with Mandolin* by the French Corot. *The Concert,* by Terborch, shows a lady playing the cello (or possibly viola da gamba) and Corot also painted a *Monk Playing a Cello.*

Renoir's *Guitar Player* is famous, as also his *Girls at the Piano.* Frans Hals gave a lute to one of his *Singing Boys* and Vermeer produced a charming *Music Lesson,* supplemented by another *Lute Player,* this time feminine. Giorgione's classic *Concert* is devoted to three singers in half length. There are of course innumerable singing and playing angels by such old masters as Fra Angelico, Botticelli, Melozzo da Forli and the della Robbias.

One might profitably study also the number of musical compositions based on famous paintings, but that is another story. We speak of "color" in music and "tone" in pictures. Unquestionably, the two arts are closely related.

Music Keeps Them Young

PEOPLE who are concerned with music, and active in any phase of the art, almost automatically remain youthful in appearance as well as behavior. The percentage of octogenarians and nonogenarians among professional musicians is truly astonishing, and even more so is the fact that so many of them have remained active in their profession long past the accepted age of retirement, and in some cases well into their eighties.

The late Arturo Toscanini remains perhaps the outstanding example of a vigorous and long-lived worker in music. He was within two months of ninety when he died in 1957 and had continued to conduct successfully almost to the end of his life.

The Finnish composer Jean Sibelius was ninety-one at the time of his death in the same year. Isidor Philipp, a great French pianist and teacher, was ninety-four when he died, playing in public occasionally even in his early nineties. The career of Gustave L. Becker, who taught the piano for many years in New York, did not end until he had reached ninety-six.

This was also the age of Mrs. Edward MacDowell, who continued to play the piano long after her husband's death, while raising funds to support the Peterborough colony of creative artists in his memory.

The English music critic and scholar Ernest Newman died not long ago at ninety, and this record was surpassed by an American writer on music, Arthur M. Abell, who in his nineties published a book of conversations with great composers.

Octogenarians are plentiful in the history of music. Two of the most famous teachers of all time, violinist Leopold Auer and pianist Theodor Leschetizky, both reached eighty-five, while the latter's best known pupil, Paderewski, came close to that mark. The British composer, Ralph Vaughan Williams, lived to the age of eighty-six, while the popular American, William C. Handy, was eighty-four when his own "St. Louis Blues" was played at his funeral in New York.

At this writing, the list of musicians still living and active in their eighties is most impressive, including the French conductor Pierre "Papa" Monteux, directing symphony orchestras at eighty-four, the composer, Igor Stravinsky, very busy still at eighty, and Pablo Casals, the great Spanish cellist and conductor, producing his annual music festivals and appearing as a soloist at eighty-three.

When one considers the fact that most musical geniuses begin their careers at an early age, often appearing in public as prodigies before reaching their teens, it may be argued that no other life work can compare with music in length of service and continued personal satisfaction. It is the music itself that keeps its practitioners young.

The Concert Business

THE managers of concert artists book their clients far ahead of time, perhaps a whole year or more in advance of their local appearances. The big names are sold almost automatically, depending only on the price. The others require a variety of effort.

Musicians fall naturally into several classes, and eventually the public may become just as aware of this as are those who deal with their business affairs.

There are only a few in the top class. They are aware of their superiority, and the best of them accept their eminence with humility, knowing that their extraordinary gifts are a mystery past explaining. They do not need to press their claims to fame, for their position is self-evident. They can ignore criticism and petty jealousies, for they are above them. They can drive hard bargains, for the demand for their services is obvious and unceasing. They are the elect of the musical world.

Just below these recognized geniuses are a number of

performers who can give honest pleasure and satisfaction to a multitude of listeners, but need some special efforts to bring them to the attention of the public and keep them in the limelight.

They deliver the goods most of the time, and any controversy as to their abilities may create good publicity in the long run. They are not self-selling, like a loaf of needed bread that has only to be pushed across the counter, but they are staple commodities, guaranteed to please the majority of their audiences, requiring only some salesmanship and promotional activity in the handling of their affairs.

In the third class are the artists for whom the concert field is a perpetual struggle. They often have ability comparable to that of the great stars, but lack the capital and consequently the management to make the most of their talents.

Their supporters may be fanatically enthusiastic, but too limited in numbers to create a real career. Sometimes there is even a question as to the commercial value of their gifts. They may be excellent musicians but lacking in the appeal of personality essential to stardom. Whatever the reason, their progress is slow and often painful. The critics give them generally favorable notices, but with reservations, and seldom the "raves" that are essential to complete success in the concert field. Many such artists envy the steady income of a good secretary.

Finally there are the would-be professionals who merely clutter up the scene and make things difficult for all concerned. Most of them should be content with being recognized as good amateurs, exercising a helpful influence for music in their communities. In some cases they are able to compete with their betters by spending money which could be used far more advantageously for the development of youthful talents requiring financial backing.

Strangely enough, these interlopers in the world of art continue to demand recognition regardless of rebuffs and obvious limitations. They get repeated opportunities to prove their worth, resulting in consistent failure. Both as interpreters and as creators they are a handicap to progress and should be eliminated from professional activity in the field of music.

Artists and Benefits

ONE sometimes wonders why any artists, and particularly musicians, ever appear in benefit shows. It is too often an unhappy experience at best.

The performer stands around, perhaps for hours, waiting to be called. He or she is often inadequately introduced, badly accompanied and barely appreciated. If the name of the performer is well known, the audience may offer respectful attention. If not, it becomes a routine matter of going through an act with little or no response.

This is particularly true of dinner-dance audiences, which have usually been stimulated to the point where they want to hear nothing but their own voices. Some individuals insist on becoming a part of the show, interrupting the artists noisily at every opportunity.

Struggling performers looking for publicity often make desperate efforts to appear on benefit programs. In most cases their work is practically wasted. Nobody remembers their names, and about all they get out of it is the MC's plea to "give this little so-and-so a great big hand."

The rudest and most insulting audiences, with the possible exception of the night club crowds, are those at benefit dinners. The fact that professional entertainers are appearing free of charge seems to encourage the well-fed-and-drunk diners to bring out their worst manners. They have paid for their tickets and contributed to a good cause, so why should they exercise any courtesy or find out what a performer may have to offer?

When a benefit concert is given in a regular auditorium, conditions are likely to be much better. But even under such circumstances, many an artist might prefer to make a financial contribution rather than be subjected to the strain of a haphazard and disorganized appearance.

After all, one would hardly expect a butcher to donate steaks and chops for charity, with some doubtful publicity the only incentive. An artist's performance is similarly his stock in trade and actually his only way of making a living.

It is true that merchants often give "door prizes" for charity affairs, and these may serve as excellent advertisements of their wares. (Occasionally there is such a plethora of these donations that practically everybody takes home a souvenir of the occasion.)

A few big benefit shows, with plenty of time in between, may be justified in any community, and for these it is always possible to secure volunteer performers of the highest calibre. But outside of these exceptions, the effort expended on lining up a program and selling tickets might better be devoted to a straightforward house-to-house campaign for funds. The artists themselves would generally prefer it that way.

Jealousy or Co-operation?

ONE of the greatest handicaps to America's musical development has been the absurd habit of local jealousies and meaningless rivalries. In too many instances, music has created discord rather than harmony. Each organization emphasizes its selfish interests and apparently resents the success of any other group, even when its activities are of a quite different character. Instead of welcoming healthy competition and joining forces whenever possible, the attitude of local musicians and music lovers has too often been that of the traditional "dog in the manger."

Of course the situation is somewhat different today from that of only a few years ago. Television, radio and records have poured an increasing amount of music into the home, and motion pictures have developed their allure on the outside. It is no longer an easy matter to gather an audience for "live" concerts or operatic performances.

Yet "canned music" will never take the place of such performances, and the real test of a community's cultural life is its ability to support artistic efforts and take an active part in them. The advice of a popular song to "accentuate the positive, eliminate the negative" applies to all such aesthetic endeavors and might well be taken to heart by all musicians, amateur as well as professional, who are seeking the favor of the public.

Every community, regardless of size, can organize at least a vocal group of some kind. A mixed chorus is the logical start for more serious music. If there are separate male and female groups, so much the better. The nucleus for such community singing will be found most logically in the various church choirs, and these should combine whenever possible in mass demonstrations of choral works.

A symphony orchestra is far more difficult to achieve, for here the personnel must be largely if not entirely professional. It is quite possible, however, in communities of average size, as has been abundantly proved.

The combination of a local orchestra, chorus and soloists logically results in opera, even when a few stars have to be imported from the nearest metropolis. Further possibilities are the various ensembles of chamber music and perhaps an old-fashioned brass band and a few jazz "combos."

Thus equipped, a community should be able to put on almost any kind of music, for the pleasure and improvement of its citizens as well as a vast civic satisfaction for its own sake. Whatever its resources may be, co-operation will always bring the best and most lasting results.

The Small-Town Orchestra

A SYMPHONY orchestra in any city of less than metropolitan proportions is bound to present some serious
problems. It is a miracle that so many of our smaller communities are able to support and maintain such a cultural
luxury today.

Admittedly, some of these orchestras have fallen by the
wayside, while others are making desperate efforts to stay
alive. Let it be admitted also that some of them do not
play too well and find it difficult to overcome the criticism
of local perfectionists who insist on comparing them with
the virtuoso organizations they hear on records and occasionally over the air.

In many cases a small-town symphony orchestra has to
be composed, at least in part, of amateurs. The professional players, especially those representing such difficult
instruments as the bassoon, the oboe and the French and
English horn, often have to be recruited from neighbor-
ing communities, perhaps even from the nearest large

city. They have only a limited time for rehearsal, and there is difficulty in bringing their numbers up to the total of eighty-five or more demanded by top symphonic standards.

Aside from the obvious challenge of assembling such an orchestra for a start, the two chief problems are those of financial support and of filling the seats at concerts, and they are by no means the same. In some communities it is not too difficult to get contributions or underwriting, but it is like pulling teeth to bring out a respectable audience. Elsewhere the local concert hall may not be hard to fill, but even a consistent sellout will still fall far short of the required revenue.

The conductor has his problems too, first of getting results from whatever performers may be available, then of arranging programs that will satisfy a majority of his listeners and finally of adapting himself to the whims and temperaments of his backers and committee members. It is not an easy life.

Some conductors, especially those of foreign birth, have tried to win favor by emphasizing American compositions, and in most cases this has resulted in dismal failure. Others have racked their brains for tricks and novelties, including "youth concerts" (which appealed equally to the adults) and an informal intimacy of presentation, often rewarded with practical success.

The ideal conductor seems to be the one who can give his programs a consistently popular appeal without ignoring either the classics or contemporary music, keeping both his patrons and his ticket-buyers happy by his selection of music and soloists, and maintaining a nice balance between artistic dignity and human understanding.

The value of a symphony orchestra to any community is unquestionable, regardless of the sneers of the snobs and the protests of the musical illiterates. Great as their educational value may be, radio and records cannot possibly take the place of personal performance, and civic pride, after the conquest of early difficulties, may eventually triumph by an achievement of greater significance than that of even a champion ball team.

Business and Art in Music

THE business and the art of music are much more closely allied than ever before. There was a time when both the artists and the teachers of music looked rather coolly upon the sincere but "commercial" efforts of the manufacturers and distributors of musical instruments, records, reproducing machines and sheet music to merchandise their products. For some strange reason, it was considered unethical to co-operate in the sale of a piano or some other expensive luxury in the musical category, although it was actually common enough, so long as it remained shrouded in secrecy.

Then the famous concert pianists began to lend their names to certain makes, mostly in return for a steady supply of instruments, but sometimes including the booking of engagements and even cash payments. (Today most of them are glad to get the use of a good piano free of charge or at the actual cost of transportation.)

It still took some time to bring the music industry and the music educators into a really close co-operation of the sort that should always have existed. The pioneer steps were taken when the music publishers, merchants and manufacturers were permitted to exhibit their wares at educational conventions for a definite price, occasionally disguised as a donation. From these experiments there developed a recognized Exhibitors' Association, which in time became the National Music Industry Council.

The relationship between the purveyors and the users of musical merchandise is now completely open, honest, forthright and healthy. The industry has discovered a tremendous market for sheet music in our schools and colleges, particularly in the band and choral fields, with a demand also for instruments of all kinds, uniforms, music stands, "raisers" and other accessories. Meanwhile, progressive directors and supervisors have taken full advantage of the many types of practical help offered by the "commercial" organizations. The latter have gradually engaged and retained educational experts to act as liaison officers for the vast army of music teachers and students. Clinics and workshops have been set up, especially in the summer months, often combining the efforts of business firms and educational institutions with gratifying results. The musical summer camp has become a recognized American institution, and here also a "commercial" background is an obvious asset.

This entire trend toward a working partnership of the art and business of music is an encouraging sign of the progress of civilization. Obviously the hardest workers in any cause are those who may reasonably expect an eventual profit of some sort. Music need not rest permanently on the vague ideal of a purely spiritual subsistence.

Be It Resolved

THERE is always a need for good resolutions, particularly in the field of music. Starting on the creative side, it is about time that our serious composers began to try for emotional expression instead of merely intellectual or mechanical, to seek honestly for something akin to inspiration and to stop being satisfied with what is primarily a technical facility. They should seek to reach a substantial public, beyond the confines of laboratory experiments, and to win the approval of more than a handful of kindred spirits, whose sincerity may be open to question.

For the popular composers, there are many possible resolutions. They should make up their minds to stop catering to a comparatively small and predominantly illiterate portion of our population, to ignore momentary quick returns and strive to achieve something of permanence even in the lighter field of music, as has been done many times and is being done today by our recognized masters of musical comedy. They should credit popular music with some elements of art and stop treating it as a rather nasty and fundamentally dishonest business. They might even make a sincere attempt to eliminate the bribery known in Tin Pan Alley as "payola" and perhaps encourage the eventual ideal of a merit system, which obviously does not yet exist.

So far as the interpreters of music are concerned, the serious artists can easily afford a few resolutions, chiefly to remind themselves that the music itself is always more important than the one who sings or plays it. They should remember that they cannot exist without creative genius to supply their material or without an audience to enjoy and appreciate it. They should resolve never to let the absurdities of temperament interfere with their integrity as artists and to maintain always a true humility in the face of a gift for which they basically deserve no credit, but which it is their duty and privilege to develop as far as is humanly possible.

The players, singers and conductors of popular music should feel a similar responsibility toward their listeners and themselves. They should ask themselves frankly what right they have to change the music of a successful composer through the effrontery known as "stylizing." They might even search their souls as to the real assets in their possession and aim at an approximation of beauty rather than a mere novelty of presentation. Some popular singers could well add a resolution to get rid of that wobble and correct the bad habit of taking a breath in the middle of a word.

For the purveyors of music by mechanical means, the

possibilities of good resolutions are enormous. The manufacturers of records and phonographs should thank
whatever gods there be for the wonderful stimuli of high
fidelity and stereophonic sound and resolve to make the
best possible use of these scientific advantages. The jukebox distributors and operators might well resolve to turn
a racket into an honest business, including the legal recognition of a creator's rights under the copyright law.

Finally, radio and television could well decide to put
their houses in order and explore the real and apparently
unsuspected possibilities of music in reaching a mass audience as well as a "quality market." They should learn a
lesson from the few programs that have been properly
presented and apply patience, fortitude and imagination
to building up standards and potentialities of which they
are still apparently unaware.

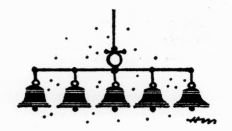

II

MORE TECHNICALLY

SPEAKING

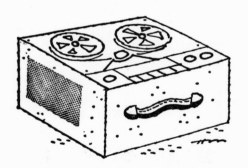

"Music by Chance"

STILL the arguments continue as to the possible significance of much of our current music, particularly the type
known to the avant-garde as "indeterminate," meaning
that it is based on pure or almost pure chance. More and
more of the world's most "advanced" composers are producing works in which the human equation plays no part
whatever, resulting in haphazard effects which can only
be described as noise.

This writer still believes in the definition of music as
"the organization of sound toward beauty," which he
enunciated some years ago. The question is just what
is meant by "beauty." The organized or disorganized
sounds now commonly inflicted upon concert audiences
may represent beauty to the ears of their creators. But is
it too much to ask that they should also have at least potentially the same effect on the listeners?

The simple truth seems to be that a new form of audible expression has arisen which is neither an art nor a

science. It might be called "experimental sound" but in most of its manifestations it is definitely not music. In fact, the emphasis today is more and more on sound as such, regardless of any inventive or inspired use of the essential elements of rhythm, melody or form. Even those who buy phonograph records of conventional music are likely to be influenced by engineering techniques rather than by the quality of a composition or the integrity of its performance.

Curiously enough, while "experimental sound" is moving steadily and relentlessly away from the long established principles of musical composition, both audiences and critics continue to be enraptured by the discovery of a comparatively unfamiliar Haydn symphony or some unsuspected example of baroque technique. (Their chief resentment seems to be aimed at the lush, romantic school of composition, which brought all the potentialities of established musical values to their highest point of expressiveness.)

It has often been argued, in defense of mechanically created sounds (including the much discussed "twelve-tone row"), that the music of Bach himself was ninety per cent mathematical. What is too often overlooked is that such a master always started with the invention of thematic material perfectly adapted to his purpose, whether a fugue, a sonata or a choral work. The weakness of "indeterminate music" lies in the purely accidental basis of its development.

In its milder forms, including electronic experiments on tape, the results may be adequately effective as "experimental sound." At its worst, the effect is inevitably that of pure nonsense.

Not long ago a New York concert program included one "composition" requiring a dishwasher, an electric blender, bottles, portable radios, two phonographs (playing different pieces) and a number of other gadgets. This was quite properly compared with the trick played by some British broadcasters who simply went about the studio banging on everything within reach and putting it on the air as "Mobile for Tape and Percussion." (The radio public and critics were completely fooled by the trick, and there were no complaints whatever.)

"Music by Chance" is even more common abroad than in America. One composer tells his performers to play whatever part of his "music" first catches their eyes. Another simply asks them to "do something completely different." Still another suggests that "the player may mimic his part, or rebel against it entirely." Some "indeterminate" music has been written in spirally bound notebooks, so that a performer can begin or end wherever he wishes, and even play the notes upside down.

These are of course extreme cases, perhaps even suggesting a tongue-in-cheek attitude on the part of their perpetrators. But it is still disquieting to find, in a machine age, the element of human communication increasingly ignored by the arts, and particularly by the most human of them all, music itself.

Mathematical Music

SOME music critics have recently expressed the opinion that the creation of serious compositions was gradually turning into an electronic or mechanical process, perhaps eventually eliminating the human equation altogether and leaving the art of music, like the science of mathematics, entirely to robots. It is a disturbing thought, but perhaps not to be taken too seriously.

While it is true that most of the "absolute music" composed today is predominantly mathematical, particularly within the formula of the "twelve-tone row," with increasing experimentation in the field of haphazard tape recording and purely artificial "gimmicks," there is unquestionably still some room for individual inspiration and at least an attempt at deliberately conceived originality.

Unfortunately the great body of American composition in the classic forms, such as the symphony, the sonata, the string quartet and the opera, has not yet succeeded in competing on equal terms with its European models. We have not yet produced a Bach, a Mozart, a Beethoven, a Brahms or a Wagner, or, for that matter, a Schumann, a Chopin, a Tchaikovsky, a Verdi or a Puccini. In view of the directions now followed by serious music, it may be doubted whether we ever shall.

But the critics should not feel too pessimistic in facing this situation. Even if contemporary composers could write in the classic and romantic styles, without merely imitating the masterpieces of the past, they probably would prefer not to do so. While it would be an exaggeration to claim that there is nothing more to be said in the established musical forms, the fact remains that today nobody seems anxious to try it. It is obviously easier to follow mathematical formulas than to trust one's own invention to create something of permanent appeal to the listener.

What is overlooked by the critics is that there are millions of Americans living today who have never yet heard a Beethoven or Brahms symphony, a Bach chorale, a Mozart opera or a Wagner music-drama. There are hundreds of great compositions, too often contemptuously dismissed as "museum pieces," which would be a revelation to the potential music-lovers of the United States if properly brought to their attention. Even those who are familiar with the so-called "standard repertoire" include a large percentage of mere sentimentalists, quite ignorant of the structural and musical significance of what they are hearing.

If these millions can be reached through radio, television, records, the screen and possibly even local concerts and operatic performances, there will be no need to cry over the surrender of serious music to a scientific age. The unlimited treasury of established masterpieces will continue to provide thrills of fresh discovery whenever a new enthusiast is added to the pioneers who have blazed the way.

The critics have a full-sized job ahead of them in guiding these various responses toward the music that has proved its permanence, and this may include the best popular and folk materials as well as recognized classics of the serious type. As long as so much great music remains undiscovered by the general public, the critics need not worry unduly. The average listener is still far from the saturation point too often reached by the professional reviewer.

Science Versus Art

SCIENCE is not only pushing music into the background of American life but in many cases taking its place. The engineers have become more important than the artists and mechanical skills are substituted for inspiration and human values.

Some composers have already arrived at the trick of aimlessly marking a sound track and accepting the haphazard results as creative music. Now the interpreters are also becoming more and more dependent on the wonders of tape recording for establishing and developing their musical reputations.

It has long been recognized that the microphone itself was responsible for a revolution in the performance of music, and particularly in the art of singing. With the coöperation of the loudspeaker, volume ceased to be a problem for either the vocalist or the instrumentalist. Voices that could hardly be heard in the average concert hall became impressively powerful through scientific amplification, and the same principle was effectively applied to such comparatively light-voiced instruments as the guitar, the accordion and the vibraphone. In the fields of recording, radio and television this was, of course, an enormous advantage.

There are people today who never heard Caruso in the flesh but are convinced of the superiority of some modern tenors merely because the up-to-date engineering techniques make them sound better on records than on the air. Similarly our popular singers often have been credited with much better voices than they actually possess, because of the scientific skill of those responsible for their broadcasting and recording.

It is now possible to build up almost any attractive youngster as a singer by mechanically supplying him with a synthetic voice. So long as the personality appeals to the teen-agers, perhaps with a "gimmick" of some sort to attract immediate attention, vocal or musical ability of any kind is of no importance.

Even our serious vocalists are given the advantages of modern tape recording by the simple device of having them sing a number several times into the helpful microphone and then splicing the tape in such a way as to combine the best features of all the interpretations in a single record.

Is it a wonder that listeners are occasionally disappointed when a singer's "live" performance fails to measure up to the records by which his or her reputation was made?

The Dual Appeal of a Classic

THE most difficult task for any creative artist, and particularly a composer of music, is to produce something that will appeal both to discriminating critics and eventually to a reasonably large public. All art that could honestly be labelled "permanent" has possessed this double appeal and continues to exercise it even after the critics themselves have forgotten their initial enthusiasm and retreated to such hackneyed terms as "old-fashioned," "dated" and "reactionary."

What is not generally realized is that it is much harder to create a work of art of such general and permanent appeal than to come up with a highly original, scientifically complex but obviously uninspired example of what has generally been called "avant-garde" or "modern" art.

In the field of music an outstanding example may be found in the compositions of the late Arnold Schoenberg. In his early days, he wrote some respectable and highly attractive pieces, such as his first string quartet and the sextet, *Verklaerte Nacht* ("Transfigured Night"). They were strongly influenced by Wagner and Richard Strauss, but they gave promise of really important creations to come. Then Mr. Schoenberg decided upon originality at all costs and found it in a completely mechanical, mathematical formula, the "twelve-tone row," representing the half-tone steps of the common chromatic scale. From then on, Schoenberg's music surrendered all claim to aesthetic significance and became a rather dull exercise in simple arithmetic. His apparently complicated works are actually far less important than a well-made sonata or symphony based upon inspired themes. Schoenberg was a great musical scholar and technician, but hardly a significant creator in the field of composition.

Such an opera as Alban Berg's *Wozzeck* was far easier to write than a supposedly conventional *Aida* or *Carmen,* not to speak of a *Meistersinger* or *Tristan*. Wagner himself said of the last-named, "As never in my life have I tasted the true joy of love, I will erect a monument to this most beautiful dream of all." And he actually succeeded in expressing sensuous love to the complete conviction of the listener, whereas all that *Wozzeck* expresses is a sordid ugliness, fortified by a few tricks of technique. This is much easier than to arrive at a Wagnerian inspiration.

As a *reductio ad absurdum,* one might mention two settings of the famous German poem, *Die Lorelei.* Franz Liszt turned its unpretentious but verbally perfect lines into an "art song," completely artificial and uninspired, merely following the obvious accents of the text and introducing a few touches of conventional drama. The song is practically never heard in this routine form. But a modest music teacher at Tübingen University, Friedrich Silcher, was inspired by Heine's words and gave them the perfect melodic setting, now known and loved all over the world. His task was more difficult than the elaborate treatment given to the *Lorelei* by Liszt, which was essentially the mechanical application of an established formula. (Too many songwriters, through the years, have suffered from the same delusion, merely following a text with correctly accented notes.)

The meeting-ground between sophisticated and naive musical tastes is not always clear. An immediate response from a mass audience may indicate nothing more than a "line of least resistance," which explains the quick success of most popular tunes. The critics themselves may be wrong in their first reactions, to be corrected ultimately by a discerning public. But when a masterpiece of any kind has achieved the status of a "classic," there is seldom real doubt as to the agreement of all honest minds and hearts.

Art Song and Folk Song

THERE has recently been a revival of interest in the so-called "art song," largely because of the performances of a few outstanding singers in this field. To many music lovers the term still has a rather vague meaning, although it should by this time be quite definite.

An art song is actually the opposite of a folk song. The latter is technically of unknown authorship, usually consisting of a number of stanzas set to one repeated melody, with only a skeleton accompaniment or none at all. An art song, on the other hand, represents the musical setting of a text of known authorship by a known composer. It is seldom stanzaic in form, the music following the words throughout, in a style the Germans call *durchkomponiert*. The accompaniment is often elaborate, perhaps as important as the melody or the words.

The model for all art song is generally found in the German *Lied,* a word which literally means "song," and should always be capitalized, like any other German noun (although critics frequently overlook this obvious fact). The nearest French equivalent is *chanson,* and examples of the form may be found also in the Italian, Spanish, Russian, Scandinavian and English languages. Basically, the principles of composition are much the same.

There are comparatively few great interpreters of art song in each generation, largely because this is a most difficult phase of the vocal art, with a correspondingly limited number of sincere and qualified appreciators. A song recitalist must be able to turn each composition into a miniature drama, without the help of scenery, costume or action of any kind. Variations of facial expression are permissible, and perhaps an occasional gesture. But otherwise the singer depends entirely on the expressiveness of the voice itself and the ability to project the meaning of the words. The skill of the accompanist is also important, and the co-operation given a singer at the piano of necessity influences the success of a concert of this type. (There was one historic occasion when the great pianist, Ossip Gabrilowitsch, accompanied the merely adequate singing of his wife, Clara Clemens, daughter of Mark Twain, with the result that the audience concentrated on the instrumental rather than the vocal significance of the recital.)

It is generally admitted that opera singers are seldom equally effective on the concert stage. If they confine themselves to operatic arias, the result may be monotony, and their training in creating broad effects of vocalism, aided by sweeping gestures, is hardly conducive to the mastery of minute detail that makes a great recitalist. There have been exceptions of course, but generally there is a fairly distinct dividing line between the stars of opera and concert.

John McCormack was a wonderful recitalist, but his operatic success was due mostly to sheer vocal beauty. Such singers as Richard Crooks and Reinald Werrenrath leaned similarly toward the concert stage. Julia Culp and Elena Gerhardt were primarily concert artists. On the other hand, Caruso gave many recitals, although his programs consisted mostly of operatic arias and folk songs. Lotte Lehmann and Lawrence Tibbett are remembered as equally successful in both fields.

Occasionally we have had successful concert singers who were widely known as "voiceless interpreters." The late Povla Frisch was one of these, an artist to her finger tips but blessed with no great vocal or physical beauty. Ludwig Wuellner, son of a Viennese music critic, was sometime accused of "talking" his songs, but with tremendous dramatic effect. Paul Draper, father of the dancer and brother of Ruth Draper, enjoyed a similar career on a smaller scale.

Today the public expects an appealing vocal quality as well as dramatic versatility from an expert in art song, while the interpreter of popular folk music can get by with an appealing personality and a clear enunciation of the text.

Songs and Songwriters

THERE is a vast difference between a songwriter and a composer in the larger sense. This applies to the serious creators of "art" songs as well as to the representatives of Tin Pan Alley.

In some ways it is actually more difficult to produce a popular song, especially if the composer writes both the words and the music, as in the case of Irving Berlin, Cole Porter, Harold Rome and Stephen Foster. The classical songwriter gets the free gift of a poem already written, and often the appeal of the finished product depends as much on the text as on the music, sometimes even more.

While there have been geniuses like Schubert, Schumann and Brahms who could glorify an often commonplace lyric by their musical setting, the great majority of the so-called art songs of the world have done little more than fit notes to words, with a meticulous regard for accent and some skill in the details of the accompaniment.

The melodic line was practically created by the text itself and seldom showed what might be considered true creative inspiration. This applies particularly to modern songwriting of the serious type, where the ideal usually seems to be little more than to give the speaking voice a series of tones of definite pitch.

Just as every illiterate amateur has the conviction that he could write a popular song if he tried, so almost every trained musician believes it is easy to set music to a well-written poem. Too often the results are just about what one would expect.

Statistics can easily be quoted to prove that the greater part of all contemporary American music is composed of songs, both serious and popular. Their creators spend a large part of their time trying to persuade singers to put them on their programs, or, better still, on records or on the air. They apparently fail to realize that if a song is to attain real success it must eventually make its way by the choice of its interpreters, not the insistence of its creators.

The Broadway publishers are quite aware of this and generally refuse to spend much time, effort or money on a song until it has given fairly good evidence of its popular appeal. They test the material in various ways, and if it does not soon become practically self-promoting, they drop it from their active list and concentrate on something else.

The more serious publishers might well take a tip from Tin Pan Alley and apply it not only to art songs but to music in the larger forms, for which no successful method of promotion has yet been devised.

Musical Accents

In vocal music with English words the details of accent and emphasis are very important. Of all the languages, English is by far the most definite in the stressing of syllables, and when these are fitted to a melody the pronunciation must be exactly the same as if the text were spoken.

Technically, no unimportant syllable or word should ever be given a strong accent, particularly the downbeat of a musical measure, and this applies to the definite and indefinite articles ("the" and "a") and to most of the one-syllable prepositions ("in," "on," "of," "by," "at," "to" etc.). It should also apply to the monosyllabic forms of the verb "to be" ("am," "is," "are" etc.) unless a special emphasis is intended. On the basis of careful workmanship, accents as well as rhymes should be avoided in the case of such suffixes as -ly, -less and -ness, although this tradition is quite widely ignored, both in verse and in musical settings.

Strangely enough, the songwriting technique of Tin Pan Alley, which permits the most atrocious assaults upon English grammar and syntax, is quite meticulous about accents, insisting that every word must be pronounced exactly as it would be if spoken instead of sung.

There are even those who claim that a popular song should never have more than one note to a syllable, which is entirely at variance with the accepted classic style. (Barbershop harmonizers do not seem to mind the rather exceptional "You're the flower *of* my heart, Sweet Adeline.")

Foreign languages, especially French and Italian, have a great advantage over English in this matter of accenting, which may be the reason why so many people consider them more singable. French words distribute their accents fairly evenly, whether spoken or sung, and a composer is given a practical carte blanche so far as musical emphasis is concerned.

The Italian language has more trailing syllables ("feminine endings") than any other, which makes it difficult to translate to music without resorting to artificial suffixes like the participial "ing." There is also considerable leeway as to accents.

German is much closer to English in its pronunciations and accents, and hence far more translatable than either French or Italian. Many a Teutonic musician has been permitted liberties of accent, as when Brahms ends the phrase *Wie bist du meine Koenigin* on an emphatic downbeat.

American listeners are frequently unaware of the mer-

its or demerits of foreign prosody, but when listening to
their own language in song their instincts generally tell
them whether the accents are right or not.

Those Descriptive Titles

THE musical public is continually fascinated by the descriptive titles attached to various familiar compositions and perhaps also unaware that many of these names did not originate with the creators of the works and might even have been indignantly rejected by them.

Probably the most famous of these unauthorized nicknames is that of Beethoven's so-called "Moonlight" sonata. The composer himself identified this popular piano piece merely as *Sonata quasi una fantasia, Op.* 27, *no.* 2. It was a critic named Rellstab who decided that the music of the opening movement reminded him of moonlight on Lake Lucerne and this led to several fanciful bits of fiction which may still be found in print.

One story was about a blind boy whose sister was playing the piano when Beethoven peeped through the window of their cottage. As a ray of moonlight entered the room, he went in and promptly improvised the sonata on the spot. Another version has Beethoven looking in at a party given by his "immortal beloved," the Countess Guicciardi, and then wandering home in the moonlight to write the sonata. There was even a motion picture which showed him improvising the sonata while another lady love was confessing her infidelity to him. (Beethoven himself admitted that this sonata might have been inspired by a poem of Seume's describing a girl in church praying for the recovery of her sick father. This rather dims the moonlight idea!)

Actually Beethoven gave titles to only two of his piano sonatas: the *Pathétique* and the *Op. 81,* whose three movements are labeled (also in French) "Farewell," "Absence" and "Return." The well-known *Appassionata* was given its name by the publisher, Cranz, as also the *Pastoral sonata.* (Beethoven himself, however, called his sixth symphony *Pastoral.* The names *Waldstein* and *Kreutzer* represent merely dedications, the first to a noble patron and the second to the violin sonata's best known interpreter. Tolstoy's story, "The Kreutzer Sonata," is in no way related to the actual music.)

Chopin is another composer whose works have often been given wholly unauthorized labels. There is the familiar "Minute Waltz," for instance, supposedly playable in exactly one minute, but actually requiring at least another half minute for its effective interpretation. It is also known as "the waltz of the little dog chasing its tail," because the whirling figure at the start suggests such a scene, as reported by George Sand. Chopin's own title was simply Waltz in D-flat, Op. 64, no. 1.

There is no real reason for calling Chopin's 9th Étude "Butterfly," although its light and airy measures may suggest the flight of that decorative insect. George Sand is again responsible for the story of the "Raindrop" Prelude, supposedly inspired by the actual sound of rain on the roof of the monastery of Valdemosa in Majorca, but Chopin himself denied this. Other fanciful Chopin titles are "Revolutionary" and "Winter Wind" for two of the Études and "Heroic" for the Polonaise now best known as "Till the End of Time."

The stories of Handel's "Harmonious Blacksmith" are pure fiction, and there is no proof that any such person existed. On the other hand, Haydn seems to have approved of the names given to some of his symphonies, particularly *The Clock, Military, Farewell* and *Surprise,* all of which are definitely justified. What is now known as the *Toy Symphony,* was called by Haydn *Kindersymphonie (Children's Symphony).* He apparently agreed to the name of *Kaiser (Emperor)* for the string quartet containing the melody later known as *Deutschland über Alles,* but originally *Gott erhalte Franz den Kaiser,* actually based upon a Croatian folk tune.

Schubert evidently permitted the title *Death and the Maiden* for a quartet and *The Trout (Die Forelle)* for a quintet, since these compositions contained variations on the melodies of the songs named. Naturally he never referred to his most popular symphony as *Unfinished.* It is probable that Mozart's *Jupiter* symphony also received its title long after the composer's death.

In general it is easier to remember names than opus numbers or key signatures, so a music lover need not be too concerned with authenticity if a musical title proves helpful in identifying a famous composition. If it makes the music more important to the listener, so much the better.

Hymns Are Good Music

Some of the best melodies in all music will be found in the familiar hymn tunes. Many of these were actually written by great composers, and even those attached to less known names often exhibit true inspiration.

For example, "Abide with Me" has a practically perfect melody, composed by the comparatively obscure W. H. Monk. It covers only six steps of the common scale and is therefore very easy to sing, making no demands whatever on the average voice. It also follows a definite rhythmic pattern and has a logical form throughout its sixteen measures.

Even more economical in its materials is that beautiful evening hymn, "Now the Day Is Over," written by Joseph Barnby to the words of Sabine Baring-Gould. In this case only four steps of the scale are required for the melody, much of the effect coming from the highly individual harmonizing. Bishop Baring-Gould also supplied the text for Sir Arthur Sullivan's "Onward, Christian Soldiers," one of the greatest march tunes of all time. Two other outstanding Sullivan melodies are "Come, ye Faithful, Raise the Strain" and "Brightly Gleams Our Banner."

America's own Lowell Mason was responsible for a number of fine hymn tunes, notably "My Faith Looks Up to Thee," "Work, for the Night Is Coming," "Safely through Another Week" and the missionary anthem, "From Greenland's Icy Mountains," with at least an arranger's credit for "Nearer, My God, to Thee."

The creators of classic masterpieces have often found their music fitted to sacred words, regardless of its original significance. The Christmas season inevitably reminds us of the rousing "Hark, the Herald Angels Sing," whose words, by Charles Wesley, are sung to a melody by Mendelssohn. The latter is responsible for several other hymns in adaptations of his familiar "Songs without Words," written originally for the piano. Christmas also draws attention to Handel's "Joy to the World," one of the most logical of all scale tunes.

The music of Haydn is heard in the popular hymn, "Oh, Worship the King," as also in "Glorious Things of Thee Are Spoken," a sacred version of the Prussian anthem, later notorious (and generally misunderstood) as *Deutschland über Alles*. This melody was originally a Croatian folk tune (appearing also in the *Kaiser Quartet*) but Haydn applied his own musical invention to "The Spacious Firmament on High," with words by the famous English writer, Joseph Addison.

The slow theme of Beethoven's *Second Symphony* was later turned into a hymn tune generally known as "Alsace." The Easter hymn, "The Strife Is O'er," goes all the way back to Palestrina. Bach is often credited with the Lenten "O Sacred Head Now Wounded," although this originated as a German folk song and reached its final development in various arrangements by the Leipzig master.

"Softly Now the Light of Day" has a fine melody by Weber, and a familiar Nocturne (*Nachtstueck*) by Schumann has served as the music for several excellent hymns. One can hear even the final theme of Sibelius' *Finlandia* sung to sacred and secular texts.

Finally there should be mention of at least two hymn tunes by Martin Luther: the immortal "A Mighty Fortress Is Our God" and the Christmas carol, "Away in a Manger." The latter is often sung to the music of "Flow Gently, Sweet Afton," supposedly a Scottish folk song but actually composed in 1838 by a Philadelphian named J. E. Spilman. "Away in a Manger" is equally effective in either setting.

The success of a good hymn depends as much on its music as on the religious significance of its words.

■■

The Importance of Percussion

THE most primitive of all musical instruments was unquestionably some sort of drum—possibly just a hollow log on which a savage beat with a stick. Rhythm is the first thing in music of which a human being is aware, and its appeal is universal.

Now this fundamental factor in the "organization of sound toward beauty" has become a favorite form of expression for the ultra-modernists. Percussion is perhaps the last word in the expression of tonal color. It represents the eternal cycle characteristic of all the arts: the simplest of all formulas in its basic patterns, developing in an endless circle of melody, harmony and form, of ever increasing complexity, until it finally returns with a new significance, as the ideal and goal of its own primitive origins.

Most of the instrumental experiments of today tend to emphasize percussion in varying degrees, and there are many compositions entirely devoted to this one form of expression. Incidentally, such up-to-date percussion has nothing whatever to do with the monotonous "big beat" of "Rock 'n' Roll" which merely competes (unsuccessfully) with the jungle rhythm itself and is utterly devoid of invention of any kind.

Regardless of individual tastes and prejudices, rhythm, normally represented by percussion of some sort, is the natural expression of our time. It reproduces the pace and spirit of life as we know it. For the illiterates it needs no ornamentation, for its function is merely that of a physical stimulus. But for the advanced musician, saturated with musical conventions of the past and seeking always a new approach to the mysteries of sound, it offers a supreme challenge in its manifold possibilities of expression.

Opera in English

TRANSLATING a foreign language into English to fit an original musical setting presents problems with which the American public is still largely unfamiliar. There has been considerable discussion of opera in English, with the naive assumption that merely translating the text into our own language will make it both intelligible and pleasing to our ears. Actually there is much more to it than that.

Let it be admitted first of all that no translation can possibly have the same effect as the original language when set to music. Translators vary in their estimates of what is most important in such a transfer of foreign thoughts and sounds. Most of them agree that a literal, word-for-word reproduction is out of the question and should be the first possibility to be dismissed. It is generally agreed also that all accents must not only fit the music perfectly but be natural to the English language.

Here is perhaps the greatest difficulty encountered by the musical translator. English prosody is very strict in its rules and traditions, whereas both French and Italian show considerable freedom of accent when sung. For instance one cannot accent the definite or indefinite article in English, but in the Latin languages it is entirely permissible. Mozart starts *Il mio tesoro* with a strong downbeat on the opening article, and Bizet produces the same effect with the article that introduces the familiar "Flower Song" in *Carmen*. But when the translator of *La Perichole* began the phrase, "A Spaniard knows" with an accent on the indefinite article, it stuck out like a sore thumb.

It has long been granted that German can be turned into English far more easily than can either French or Italian, simply because German and English possess the same roots and many similarities in vocabulary, while French and Italian derive from Latin and have very little in common with our own language.

The horrors of literal translation are illustrated in many of the librettos still sold in our opera houses, and these absurdities are surpassed by the translations from French and Italian heard by German audiences. (They do not seem to mind this, any more than the Latin races mind an emasculated Wagner in their own languages.)

What is really important is that the original vowel sounds be reproduced as far as possible, for practically every note of vocal music is represented by a vowel. Rhymes are of comparatively little importance and should never be allowed to interfere with accent or fidelity of sound and meaning. A blanket order for the mere substitution of one language for another is not enough.

Basic Patterns of Melody

Musical scholars have spent much time and effort in trying to analyze the appeal of melody and to explain why a certain pattern of notes has a consistently favorable effect on the average listener, while the same notes, in a slightly different arrangement, may make no impression whatever. (Actually, this eternal problem has lost much of its significance as a result of the melodic vagaries of most contemporary music.)

A "tune detective" who listens carefully to the successful melodies of all time almost of necessity arrives eventually at certain basic patterns which repeat themselves endlessly, perhaps with entirely different effects, depending on the rhythmic and harmonic treatment, the instrumentation and the technical form involved. The commonest of such basic patterns may be found in the tones of the common major chord and the equally familiar major scale. Practically every melody of established permanence can thus be analyzed in terms of the chord or the scale or a combination of the two.

Consider first the pattern of the major chord, consisting of the first, third, fifth and eighth notes in the major scale. These are the natural tones of such an instrument as the bugle, and practically all the bugle calls of the world are built upon this universal progression of 1,3,5,8. They are familiar in the rapid tempo of "Reveille" as well as the slow and mournful "Taps," plus many others, often extended to full-length marching melodies. As a logical result one finds the notes of the bugle in a majority of the great patriotic and martial airs of all countries.

If you play the opening phrase of our own "Star-Spangled Banner" ("Oh, say can you see") you are using the bugle pattern in an inverted sequence. By sounding those four tones together on the piano, you actually arrive at a perfect major chord. You may then make the startling discovery that the same four tones, in the slightly different sequence of 5,1,3,5,5,3,5,8, create the opening phrase of Germany's "Watch on the Rhine," known also as "Bright College Years," Yale's Alma Mater.

The three most important tones of the pattern, in the order of 5,3,1, appear near the start of the old Russian Czarist Anthem, familiar to Americans as "Hail, Pennsylvania" and as a hymn tune. The French Anthem "Marseillaise" shows the same three-note sequence, an octave higher, in the opening phrase. George M. Cohan used the bugle tones deliberately in his patriotic "Over There," and they appear also at the start of "The Long, Long Trail," another hit song of the first World War.

Irving Berlin naturally brought them into his "Oh, How I Hate to Get Up in the Morning," and they can still be heard in one of the most familiar of the automobile horn-calls.

The pattern of the major scale is just about as common in music as that of the major chord. Handel provided an excellent example of a downward scale sequence at the start of his Christmas carol, "Joy to the World." In fact, that fine melody sticks to scale sequences throughout, except for one octave jump near the close. The same composer favored the major scale in his popular "Largo" (actually an operatic aria), as well as in many parts of the *Messiah*. Tchaikovsky opens the Finale of his *Fourth Symphony* with a similar descending scale passage, leading up to the Russian folk song "The Birch Tree," which is actually a complete scale tune, but in minor key.

An old American popular song was called "Ragging the Scale," and it fully lived up to its title. Another hit of the past, "No Wedding Bells for Me," imitated a scale progression of the chimes, twice following the octave downward. In "The Birth of the Blues," the accented notes of the melody simply followed the scale upward. A more recent scale tune in the popular field was called "I Believe," successfully suggesting the universality of this sentiment by its emphasis on a universal musical pattern.

These are only a few examples of what might be called an established habit with composers of all kinds, and they offer a good reason for the fact that so many melodies have a way of sounding similar to the average ear. A close observer of melodic patterns is likely to find such an approach of real value in following the details of even a classic symphony. Brahms, for example, was fond of constructing themes from the notes of the major chord. (His *Violin Concerto, Second Symphony* and the song, *Sapphic Ode,* all start with a melody based on the chord of D major.) Mozart was more partial to scale progressions, and Beethoven used both patterns with equal effect. It is fascinating to follow the "Fate" motto through the entire first movement of his great *Fifth Symphony* and to discover that it consists of only two tones, representing the interval of the major third, with a rhythmic pattern now interpreted as "V for Victory."

On Reading Notes

Why is it that so few people ever learn to read music? Lots of them pretend to, but even in the respected choral societies, there are not many singers who can actually read a line of melody at sight. They learn the notes more or less by rote, after starting with a vague idea of what goes up and what goes down.

To read a piece of music as one reads a magazine or a newspaper is not really difficult at all, and there is a definite pleasure in being able to know how a composition should sound, without the technique to play it on the piano or any other instrument. After all, the little dots and ovals hanging on a fence represent definite sounds, just like the words and letters on a printed page.

Practically anyone can read those symbols without having to pronounce them out loud, and this should be even easier with printed music. For the musical alphabet contains only seven letters, from A to G inclusive, in comparison with the English alphabet of twenty-six letters.

Moreover, the combinations of musical letters in melody or harmony always sound the same, instead of offering the variety of possible pronunciations that are apparent in English.

Anybody can learn to read music fluently and accurately without playing a note on an instrument of any kind. One learns by simply doing it, just as one learns to spell and read one's own language. The letters can be mastered in five minutes. After that, one must use them in a practical fashion until their interpretation in sound becomes automatic. The normal process is to learn music by ear, as one learns a language, and then gradually to master the reading, writing and spelling of that language.

The widespread inferiority complex about note-reading has held back an enormous number of potential music lovers, many of whom try to make a virtue of this absurd handicap. They boast of playing entirely by ear and being "unable to read a note," which is the same as expressing pride in the fact that one can get the news of the day and the literature of all time only by hearing it recited out loud. For anyone with eyes to see, this is ridiculous.

The most absurd mistakes are constantly made by artists who seem unaware of the definite meaning of musical notes. Christmas cards continue to appear with musical notes that make no sense at all.

The greatest fallacy concerned with the writing of notes is in the field of composition. Those who don't know how to write music point to Irving Berlin and feel that they must have the same kind of ability. Those who do know how (including some fairly good composers) argue that the mere command of notation is a guarantee of inspiration. They are both completely wrong.

Music Must Communicate

THIS writer long ago defined an artist as one who succeeds in transferring his own thoughts, moods and emotions to others through his command of a means of communication. Anyone at all may quite sincerely experience thoughts, moods and emotions, but this does not make him a creative artist. It is only when he has mastered a technique that sooner or later inevitably conveys his experience to others that he can honestly lay claim to any such distinction.

This is the real impasse faced by contemporary music. Unquestionably, many of our serious composers are entirely sincere in expressing themselves, and there is no denying their possession of an elaborate technique which in their own minds probably constitutes a means of communication. With equal certainty it may be claimed that most of this material is cordially hated by the average listener and that even its apparently enthusiastic supporters are far too often indulging in a peculiar combination of hypocrisy and snobbery. (This estimate eliminates the most extreme cases of obvious nonsense, aiming merely at novelty for its own sake and having little or nothing to do with music as such.)

That the best of contemporary musical composition represents a technical advance over the established classics is undeniable. Whether or not this constitutes an improvement, however, is open to question. What we hear today is certainly a different although not necessarily a better music than was written in the past.

It may be worth noting that the most sincere and effective exponents of the current style of composition are just as enthusiastic about a recognized classic and probably just as effective in its interpretation. It is sometimes hard to believe that such a conductor as Leonard Bernstein can be so completely thrilled by a Haydn or Mozart symphony and then, perhaps on the same program, exhibit the same ecstasy over the work of a Berg or a Webern, which to many a listener sounds simply awful. (In this case one is forced to assume that Mr. Bernstein actually loves every type of music that seems to him supremely well done in its particular style.)

One result of the attitude practically forced upon musical interpreters as well as critics by today's composers is that almost every work of long standing in the repertoire comes to be regarded as "old hat," no longer to be taken seriously, regardless of the manifest preferences of the public. Actually this is far from true. What the critics and many of the artists themselves resent is the weak imitation of a style that in its highest form is admittedly immortal. They do not really object to the style itself, but rather to its application to commonplace materials, lacking the inspiration of true genius. The composer of today has acquired an actual terror of the word "diatonic" and is inclined to shy at even "chromatic" or "impressionistic." This often implies a lack of confidence rather than of ability. Music written in the new style is sure at least to sound "different," and it may be years before its aesthetic value can be properly appraised.

Musical Traditions

THE word "tradition" turns up frequently in spoken and written comments on music. Some people are still not quite sure of just what it means.

Actually "tradition" implies the acceptance of a habit— "the way it has always been done." It is not necessarily a compliment to call the interpretation of a piece of music "traditionally correct." For while the tradition may uphold the composer's original intention, it may also represent merely a way of singing or playing certain passages arbitrarily fixed by an authority years ago and continued largely because later interpreters were either too lazy or too ignorant to express any ideas of their own.

Mozart's compositions are particularly exposed to tradition, and fortunately the composer himself left some fairly definite instructions as to style, tempo, ornaments, "rubato" (rhythmic freedom), etc. There are also the writings of his contemporaries to suggest details of interpretation that may be considered authoritative.

In too many quarters, however, a Mozart tradition still persists which labels his music "dainty," "charming," "naively delightful," "mathematically correct," "a series of formal patterns" or "a classic model of tonal design," often at the expense of its human, dramatic and emotional qualities. Conductors like Bruno Walter and Sir Thomas Beecham worked valiantly to break down such traditions, and their performances of Mozart have frequently been called a "revelation" by both critics and audiences.

Lawrence Tibbett used to tell about one of his battles with tradition at the Metropolitan Opera. When he first sang the role of Scarpia in Puccini's *Tosca,* he felt that this suave villain should appear informally in his home surroundings of the second act, without the white wig and elaborate costuming of his first entrance in the Roman church. It was a sufficiently logical idea, but the critics and public would have none of it. Some of them even failed to recognize Scarpia in his natural hair and wondered whether a new character had suddenly been introduced into the opera! Mr. Tibbett quickly gave up his brief revolt against tradition and settled for the accepted interpretation of the role, visually as well as vocally.

Today the Metropolitan Opera is indulging in many departures from tradition, sometimes to good effect and occasionally to a chorus of criticism. The management has been accused of unnecessarily distorting some of the old war horses which would be automatic winners under almost any conditions. It has been argued that new productions are practically wasted on such sure-fire operatic material as *Faust, Carmen, Aida, Rigoletto* and the twin bill of *Cavalleria Rusticana* and *Pagliacci.*

Let it be admitted in any case that the most extreme innovations at the Metropolitan are still mild when compared with what Wieland and Wolfgang Wagner have done to the traditions of their grandfather's music dramas at Bayreuth.

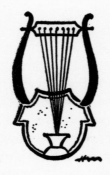

The Mystery of Inspiration

THE word "inspiration" is still a stumbling block to those who try to write or talk about music, particularly in its more serious forms. Apparently it is an element which the general public unerringly discovers in time, but which is very difficult, if not impossible, to explain or analyze, much less to detect at a first hearing. Eventually, as one becomes aware of a definitely inspired musical passage or composition, a feeling of inevitability is created, but how the composer arrived at this remains a mystery.

Perhaps critics and music lovers in general should be satisfied with explaining the details of technique, dissecting form, harmony, instrumentation, etc., and taking the quality of inspiration for granted, if only because a work has proved its permanent appeal to the human ear. It would obviously be dangerous to argue that the inherent value of a musical creation is in direct ratio to the extent of this appeal. Too many compositions have arrived at an almost universal popularity chiefly because they represent an obvious "line of least resistance."

Nevertheless it can safely be stated that the truly great inspirations of all art, and particularly of music, have in time achieved wide recognition, and that their established permanence entitles them to the highly prized label of "classics." The more one studies the classics of music, the more one leans toward the conviction that the basic element of inspiration lies in melodic invention plus the musicianship to make the most of it. Every recognized classic in musical literature combines these essential factors, even when the listener is quite unaware of their significance.

Composers have arrived at such results in two ways. In most cases the fundamental melodic idea has been in effect a spontaneous creation, to be worked out with the most painstaking application of technical knowledge and inventiveness, in line with Carlyle's definition of genius as "the infinite capacity for taking pains." (The popular delusion that a complete composition leaps magically from a creative brain is of course completely absurd.)

The less common method of musical creation applies painstaking thought and endless experimentation even to the invention of a basic theme, and here the famous sketch-books of Beethoven are a significant guide to the working habits of a genius. It is most enlightening to study these experiments of a melodic master, who was apparently never quite satisfied with the results of his efforts. Two outstanding examples of this painstaking approach are the sketches for the slow movements of the

Fifth Symphony and the *Emperor Piano Concerto*. The first was initially conceived as a rather commonplace scale progression, later suggested in the variations but not in the inspired melody itself. What finally became the deeply moving slow theme of the concerto started as a similarly conventional series of scale patterns. The gradual progress from the obvious to the inevitable is in both cases an astonishing revelation.

Richard Wagner evidently had his own system of arriving at exactly what he wanted, especially in searching for a *Leitmotiv*. Take, for instance, the theme identifying the hero of Wagner's sacred music-drama *Parsifal*. Here, in a series of only nine tonal combinations, the composer establishes not only the character of Parsifal but the basic idea of the entire opera. The first three notes, on the words *durch Mitleid*, suggest by their slight dissonance a confused sympathy, clarified immediately by the simple harmony of *wissend* ("knowing") and then proceeding to an exalted conclusion on *der reine Tor* ("the pure fool"). When Wagner reaches the ineffable mood music of the "Good Friday Spell," he again achieves the effect of inevitability. Incidentally, his use of the traditional "Dresden Amen" for the most solemn moments of the ritual might also be considered an inspiration.

How can one explain the infallible appeal of Schumann's "The Poet Speaks" at the close of his *Scenes From Childhood* or the similar passage concluding the song cycle, *Woman's Love and Life?* What is the secret of the brass chorale in the Finale of Brahms' *First Symphony*, when, according to the late Lawrence Gilman, "the heavens open"? These and many other climactic moments are the best answer to the current belief that significant music can be written without inspiration.

III

FOR AMATEURS, PARENTS
AND CHILDREN

Amateurs Versus Professionals

THE difference between musical amateurs and professionals is very great. This applies to both creative and interpretive talents and is almost as obvious in popular as in serious music.

For some reason a vast number of would-be composers have acquired the belief that if they know how to write notes that make sense they are automatically fired with inspiration, which is the same as arguing that anyone able to write the English language is potentially a best-selling novelist or playwright. Curiously enough, the opposite argument is also used by aspiring musical novices. They point to Irving Berlin's and George M. Cohan's supposed ignorance of notation and claim that since they share the same ignorance, they must also be logical producers of hit songs.

An astonishing number of manuscripts are sent out by such hopeful amateurs which reveal not only a complete unawareness of the fundamentals of music but also an apparent disregard of the principles of songwriting, as illustrated by current hits as well as the established "standards" of the past. Aside from the musical illiteracy of their compositions, they write in a style that was already out of date at the beginning of this century.

These deluded souls also fail to realize the nature of the music publishing business as it is today. They do not grasp the fact that getting a song into print means practically nothing. It can be done by anyone at his own expense. But there the matter will end unless someone, preferably a recognized music publisher, is willing and able to spend a considerable sum in bringing the song to the attention of the public. Primarily this promotion consists of getting the song recorded and played on the air and on jukeboxes. This is accomplished largely through the system of bribery known as payola. Without one or more effective recordings, consistently "plugged" by the disk jockeys, even a good song will get nowhere commercially. The professional songwriter accepts this situation as a matter of course.

The problems of the serious composer are entirely different. He is fortunate if he gets any public performances or recordings, and if he writes in the contemporary idiom, his appeal to the average audience is very doubtful. Publication is a luxury, and even the distribution of orchestral works on a rental basis is not easily achieved. In this field the amateur has absolutely no chance unless he is extraordinarily gifted and willing to devote years to intensive study, with the probability of making his living in other ways after all and pursuing his creative work as a side line.

Among the interpreters of instrumental music there is a similar gulf between amateurs and professionals, and this applies not only to pianists, violinists and cellists but to symphonic conductors as well. Success in these fields is reserved for a few unquestioned geniuses, and again substantial sums must be spent in promotion and advertising, regardless of "rave" notices (which are the only ones to make any impression on the public).

Singers, however, apparently live in a different world, in which the merit system has no place. There seems to be an unending stream of voiceless, untrained youngsters whose dead-pan delivery of illiterate material somehow appeals to listeners of their own age. The absurdities of Rock 'n' Roll have made such artificial careers all the more common. Even on the higher levels of concert and opera, a singer occasionally wins success through qualities unrelated to music as such. There have also been cases of amateurs' temporarily holding the limelight by merely spending plenty of money and giving away free tickets. Their wealth would have been far better spent in subsidizing some real talents lacking financial resources.

In view of the hardships, frustrations and disappointments in the life of a professional musician, one sometimes wonders why so many amateurs continue to strive for a similar ordeal. They could probably make a better living as clerks or stenographers, and if they are merely looking for compliments they can get their full share without ever competing with the professionals. Actually we need good musical amateurs far more than adequate professionals, and their enthusiastic activities can be a real blessing to the communities which they serve.

On Debut Recitals

Every year aspiring musicians of all kinds tempt fate and the New York critics by giving debut recitals, mostly in Town Hall or the large or small auditoriums of Carnegie Hall. In many cases one wonders why they take the chance. Yet often these experimental concerts are justified, even though they may result in nothing more than perfunctory notices by second-string reviewers.

These comparatively unknown artists should ask themselves a few searching questions before hiring a New York hall and demanding the attention of perhaps the most critical and sophisticated audience in the world today, not to speak of the usually satiated and blasé critics. What equipment is expected of a singer or instrumentalist daring to present an entire program of solos, with only an accompanist for support?

First of all, it should be realized there must be no technical flaws of any kind. These are all too easily detected even by inexperienced listeners. A vocalist dare not sing

flat or sharp, or under an obvious strain, with a pronounced wobble or an unpleasant quality of tone. A violinist or cellist is expected to meet the same standards of
technique, with additional demands on digital dexterity
and even greater expectations of tonal beauty. A pianist
is permitted only a small number of errors, again all too
obvious even to the average hearer, and once more there
is a demand for brilliance of execution, plus whatever
beauty of tone the instrument permits.

All this is taken for granted in the heated competition
among concert artists of our time. There are far too many
who possess a practically perfect technique to permit any
performer with inferior equipment to make much of an
impression on the public. But this technical perfection is
only the starting-point.

Assuming that a recitalist is free from any blatant errors such as faulty intonation or slipshod fingering, and
manifests an appealing tone and an attractive personality,
there remains the problem of interpretation, and this presents the real test for an artist, regardless of technical skill.
Those elusive qualities known as musicianship and style
are absolutely essential to acknowledged success on the
concert stage.

On the whole this means chiefly carrying out the intentions of the composer of each work. These may not always
be entirely clear even to experienced and well-trained
musicians. (In the popular field the distortions practiced
by the so-called "song stylists" automatically deprive them
of any possible claim to artistry.)

There are ways of conveying an atmosphere of indi-
viduality to an audience without insulting or ignoring the

creative significance of a musical composition. The truly great interpreter of great music inevitably establishes a conviction of integrity, while making every performance uniquely his own. The musical public recognizes such transcendent art and insists upon it as a complement to an absolutely secure technical basis. These ideals must be realized by every musician sincerely desiring a significant career.

The Deluded Amateur

WE are often told amateur musicians should perform for their own satisfaction, and occasionally the opinion is hazarded that they might also give some pleasure to their friends. Such encouragement, however, has not always produced happy results.

There is a species of musical amateur that seems to glory in creating acute misery in captive listeners, and the worst offenders in this respect are people who give parties and then insist that their guests listen to their own horrible singing or playing. Nobody likes to be impolite in such cases, for obviously the effort is a worthy one. But why inflict suffering needlessly?

It is hard to believe that some of these amateurs are unaware of how bad they really are, and one can only hope that sooner or later someone will tell them the truth. Strangely enough, they seem to enjoy especially performing for professionals, perhaps in the vague belief that this will somehow result in a job.

Singers are the worst offenders, perhaps because their shortcomings are most obvious even to inexperienced listeners. Nobody can fail to be aware of a note that is clearly out of tune, or afflicted with a wobble or of raucous quality. But many a would-be vocalist, sublime in his or her self-confidence, apparently assumes that such defects are not really noticeable.

The classic instance of a career of excruciatingly bad singing was that of a lady named Florence Foster Jenkins. She supported a music club in New York, and one of the penalties of membership was listening to her in at least one concert a year.

In time the members discovered that these events were uproariously funny and punctuated the entire program with hearty laughter in the face of their patroness. Mrs. Jenkins evidently took this as a compliment and finally decided to give a recital in Carnegie Hall, when she was already in her seventies. She persuaded a manager to handle the details, and to the surprise of everyone concerned it was a sellout.

Those lucky enough to be present will never forget the occasion. The climax came in the Jenkins interpretation of the familiar "Clavelitos" ("Carnations"), during which the singer strewed artificial flowers all over the stage from a basket under her arm. There was tremendous applause at the end, whereupon she had her accompanist gather up all the carnations and put them back in the basket, after which she repeated the entire performance!

Some records were made of the Jenkins voice (one was heard on an "Information Please" broadcast), eventually brought out by RCA Victor and now a collector's item.

Unfortunately, Florence Foster Jenkins died only a few weeks after her Carnegie Hall triumph, immortalized as perhaps the worst voice of all time.

Occasionally one wonders whether all those "artists" who hire a hall and insist on giving a concert are aware of how high professional standards are today. Often they would better spend their money by backing real and youthful talents, most of whom need financial support while establishing the reputation they deserve.

How to Become a Music Critic

THE subject of music criticism is fairly sure to create violent controversy, with artists and managers generally agreeing on its uselessness, except when they are enjoying favorable reviews.

The question most commonly asked of those in the profession is "How does one get to be a music critic?" A good answer might be "By getting on a newspaper." Music critics are seldom engaged as such, particularly in our smaller communities. They are developed from other jobs, even those of office boys or copy readers. Among the great music critics of the past, William J. Henderson was first known as an expert on yachting, while Henry E. Krehbiel covered the police courts and baseball in Cincinnati before coming to New York. The important thing is to be on hand when the opportunity arises. A city editor will often turn to almost any willing and promising young man or woman on his staff if a musical performance is to be covered at short notice. Frequently such work is done by a society editor, and some of our best critics outside of New York are equipped to write about the theatre and movies as well as music. It is an accepted fact that successful sports-writers have often become excellent reviewers of both drama and music.

The next question is "How should a music critic go about his work?" to which could be added such further inquiries as "How severe may a critic be in his condemnation of a bad performance and how lavish in his praise of a good one?" "How many technical terms are permitted in a review aimed at the average reader?" and finally "Just what is meant by 'constructive' criticism?" The answers to these questions are not as simple as might be supposed.

First of all, a music critic should remember always that what he writes is never more than a personal opinion. If that opinion is based upon considerable knowledge, good taste and a sincere love of music, so much the better. It nevertheless remains an opinion, with which many music-lovers of equal knowledge, taste and sincerity may quite honestly disagree. No critic is infallible in his judgment, as history has repeatedly and embarrassingly proved.

This writer's rule was always to forget that he was a critic when attending a performance and to consider himself merely a member of the audience. At the end of the program he would try to analyze his reactions, good or bad, and then put them into words that anyone could presumably understand. It is far easier to exploit one's scholarly background or deal in abstruse technical terms than to interpret an unprejudiced response to musical beauty in a stimulating and intelligible fashion.

The worst music critics are those who cannot resist the

temptation to show off, making themselves the protagonists of their reviews instead of the artists whose work they are supposedly reviewing. Nearly as offensive as these exhibitionists are the critics who hesitate to express any decided opinion, either good or bad. They balance every compliment with "on the other hand" and seem utterly unable to express either wild enthusiasm or bitter disappointment. (It should be remembered also that a good critic always hopes for a good performance and would much rather praise than condemn.)

This brings up the final question as to "constructive criticism," which to most artists seems to mean a "rave notice." Actually a review is constructive if it points out how a performance might have been improved instead of merely calling it inadequate. It is as simple as that.

Certainly a music critic does not have to be in any sense a performer himself, although some practical experience may be considered helpful. If he can escape the curse of omniscience and remember that he is expressing no more than an honest opinion, he may end by doing music a real service.

Pleasure or Drudgery?

Music educators are continually talking about "theory" and "applied music." What they mean is the difference between analytical listening and actual participation in the art.

For some reason, it is argued that only those who have taken some part in music can really appreciate it, and this participation is generally defined in the categories of playing in a string quartet, performing creditably on the piano or some other instrument, or being a vocal soloist. Such impossible ideals have proved an immeasurable handicap to the development of a real musical life in America.

The old-fashioned piano teacher treated every pupil as a potential artist. Regardless of talent or ambition, the defenseless youngsters of a past generation were compelled to practice scales and exercises *ad infinitum,* often becoming active enemies of music instead of the music lovers they should have been. Most of those children are grown-up now and confess that after "taking" for years they were still unable to play a comparatively simple composition adequately. The youthful students of the piano were generally doomed to mediocrity at best and hardly any of them could honestly aspire to a real musical skill. Then what was the object of all this unnecessary drudgery? Why should music have been made a task and a duty instead of the normal and logical pleasure that it should be?

Even today there is undue emphasis on skilled performance, particularly in our schools and colleges. Bands, orchestras and choruses are trained to the limit of their capacities in a futile pursuit of perfection. Contests and competitions of all kinds are used as an incentive to intensive rehearsal, often resulting only in frustration and heartaches.

Instead of becoming familiar with a substantial amount of the literature of music, these students concentrate on a limited repertoire in which they eventually invite comparison with professional organizations. Their teachers and coaches are judged not by the enthusiasm they may have created, but by the standards of public performance in a few show pieces to which they have devoted months of time and effort.

The irony of it all is that the majority of these young performers make little or no effort to keep up their music after graduation from school or college. They do not even support local orchestras and choral societies, much less take part in their activities.

The answer to the problem may lie in a far wider participation in music on a far lower level of achievement. Millions of comparatively untalented persons could enjoy performing unpretentiously on an instrument of some sort or singing in a community chorus just for the fun of it, without any ambition to astonish their companions. And they would be all the more appreciative of the work of a great artist as a result of these modest efforts.

Our Musical Presidents

ONE hardly expects to find much musical talent among our presidents of the past, but the average is perhaps higher than is generally realized.

Francis Hopkinson, a signer of the Declaration of Independence and our first important composer, dedicated a collection of his songs to George Washington when the latter was about to assume the presidency. In acknowledging the dedication, Washington wrote to the composer, "I can neither sing one of the songs, nor raise a single note on any instrument to convince the unbelieving." Yet there is a picture of our first president in the Mt. Vernon collection which shows him playing the flute, and he is known to have had one or two keyboard instruments in his home. At least there were many songs written *about* George Washington, and the composition known as the "President's March," by Philip Phile of Philadelphia, eventually became the patriotic song, "Hail Columbia,

Happy Land," with words by Francis Hopkinson's son Joseph.

John Adams was credited with possessing a guitar, a harp and a piano, but there is no evidence that he could play any of them. He too was honored by a famous song, "Adams and Liberty," whose melody was the same as that of "The Star-Spangled Banner," fitted to a text by Robert Treat Paine, son of the famous Thomas Paine.

History records that Thomas Jefferson was an excellent musician, certainly the best among all of our presidents, in addition to other artistic talents. He was unquestionably an outstanding amateur violinist, sometimes getting up at five in the morning to practice. His wife played the spinet, and they often made music together, occasionally inviting friends to join them, and his letters show that he looked forward to eventually organizing an informal orchestra at Monticello.

John Tyler reputedly wrote both the words and the music of a serenade, dedicated to his wife. Millard Fillmore was considered an ardent music lover, but hardly a performer.

It was Abraham Lincoln who first drew attention to the possibilities of the modest harmonica or "mouth organ," which he called his "little brass band," with a sly dig at the real band used by Stephen Douglas during their historic debates. Lincoln loved our simple folk songs and dances, and was equally responsive to the stately "Battle Hymn of the Republic" and the lively measures of "Dixie," which he declared the property of the entire country after the end of the War between the States.

Woodrow Wilson had some musical ability, singing in

a good tenor voice and occasionally indulging in a tap dance in his Princeton home. As an undergraduate at the University (Class of 1879) he was listed as a member of the glee club.

Warren G. Harding was definitely a musical president, playing a number of band instruments with considerable skill, both in ensemble and as a soloist. Calvin Coolidge was not a performer, but had an honest interest in music, stimulated by his wife, and actually delivered a scholarly address on the subject in Boston, on the occasion of the Chickering centennial. (It is now credited to a ghost writer.)

Franklin D. Roosevelt had a wide range of musical tastes, and his successor, Harry Truman, still preserves his reputation as a pianist, based largely upon his playing of the Paderewski "Minuet," which he assures his listeners is *not* the same as Beethoven's easier one in G. (When Mr. Truman once joined trumpet-playing Czar Petrillo of the Musicians' Union in an impromptu TV duet, the results were not too happy.)

The harmonica emerges once more as the instrument favored by Dwight Eisenhower for personal performance. President Kennedy and his wife are both musically inclined and honestly interested in all the arts, as they have repeatedly proved in practical fashion. There will always be some music in the White House, if it is only the U. S. Marine Band playing "Hail to the Chief." But an administration dedicated to the advancement of our culture can have a positive influence on American music.

Children and Music

ONE of the commonest questions asked by parents is "How early should I start my child's musical education?" The answer is "As soon as possible after birth."

Obviously a child should hear a great deal of music before attempting to play an instrument or even to sing. This earliest musical experience may well be supplied by the mother herself, who should at least be able to hum a simple lullaby. She has the advantage of knowing that her baby is too young to be critical, and by the time her offspring can check up on her musical ability it may have become quite adequate, developing simultaneously with the child's own taste and education.

Of course the best way to bring music immediately to the attention of a child is through phonograph records. Parents are strongly advised to provide their children with turntables of their own quite early in life. It is astonishing how quickly they can learn to make use of these practical aids to musical enjoyment. Long before they have learned to read, it will be noticed that little boys and girls can mysteriously and unerringly pick out their favorite records and either ask to have them played or put them on the turntable themselves.

These early pieces can be of the simplest type: nursery rhymes established by tradition, folk songs with familiar melodies, marches and other examples of regular rhythm. Babies have been known to kick rhythmically to the sound of music before they could walk, and the ability to carry a tune before talking is quite common.

Before long the average child will be humming or singing along with the records, eventually also marching and dancing in time to their music, and the next logical step is that of trying to imitate these pleasant sounds on musical toys or simple instruments of some sort. (These observations are not mere theories, but based upon actual experience.)

Fortunately the record industry is now well aware of the constant need of special material aimed at children of various ages. The catalogues of the music dealers as well as many book stores contain comprehensive lists of successful recordings carefully prepared for this rapidly growing and highly significant market.

While children's records may sometimes be unduly influenced by television, movies and comic books, there is a vast library available of wholesome and consistently entertaining material adapted to every age and taste. The parents' problems really begin after their children submit to the ordeal of taking music lessons. In too many cases youthful enthusiasm is killed by the old-fashioned teacher's insistence on turning the lessons into drudgery.

Musical Prodigies

THE problem of the musical prodigy continues to plague many persons who are sincerely interested in the progress of the art. Let it be admitted that practically every musician of note in all history was a *Wunderkind,* precociously exhibiting an amazing talent, even genius, at a tender age. In most cases, however, these extraordinary gifts were kept secret from the general public until the prodigy had attained an age that justified professional exploitation.

In a few instances, a musically talented child was exploited long before reaching what could be considered maturity, and sometimes this had the effect of snuffing out a potentially promising career. But there are enough cases on record where wise parents and friends managed to hold back a prodigy until the stage of mere technical facility had been passed. Meanwhile, vitally necessary instruction in musicianship was supplied and a dependable repertoire developed for consistent success on the concert stage.

The classic example of such treatment of musical precociousness was Josef Hofmann, who after playing in public from the age of 6 to 10 retired for two years of intensive study with Anton Rubinstein, and eventually became the leading pianist of his day. Similar judgment was exercised in the case of Yehudi Menuhin, whose childhood virtuosity on the violin astonished every listener, but who wisely studied with Enesco and others before entering upon a real career of consistent success. His juvenile contemporary, Ruggiero Ricci, was the victim of unfortunate circumstances in his childhood, but eventually also arrived at an impressive musical maturity.

Ruth Slenczynska was almost ruined by a tyrannical and vainglorious father, but survived a tragic youth and is today enjoying a career of solid achievement and public approval. On the other hand a little boy named Richard Korbel, who created an early sensation climaxed by a Hollywood contract, seems to have disappeared from the musical horizon and may have been permanently lost to the concert field.

Van Cliburn may prove the exception to the rule, for he has appeared in public fairly steadily since early childhood, winning prizes and awards in every direction. Yet even this phenomenal young man took time for some serious work with Rosina Lhevinne at the Juilliard School of Music before leaping into the limelight by way of Moscow's Tchaikovsky competition.

The parents of musical prodigies need not worry unduly about the normal development of these exceptional gifts, which must be revealed early if at all. It is their premature exploitation that should be avoided.

"Music for Fun"

Too many educators appear to believe that "music for fun" suggests turning all study of the art into mere recreation. Some of them go so far as to claim that if such study is honestly enjoyable it cannot have any real educational value. They insist that school or college students playing in bands and orchestras or singing in choral groups must undergo the drudgery demanded by standards of perfection, limiting themselves to a small repertoire at close to a professional level instead of exploring the vast literature available in their field and adequately performing a great variety of music for their own pleasure.

The same perfectionists who insist upon turning practice into drudgery are inclined to regard with suspicion the type of music teaching aiming at a so-called "appreciation" (a word for which "enjoyment" should long ago have been substituted). They cannot believe that any course of study that is honestly enjoyable can represent significant mental discipline and they spend much time and effort looking for ways to make such a course as dull, difficult and technical as possible, avoiding with horror the possible accusation that students of "appreciation" or "general music" are merely having the fun of listening to records of the classics.

But is there any law of pedagogy against making any course of study enjoyable? And is education to be limited to subjects that may be expected to have a professional or commercial significance in the future life of every student?

Why, after all, should music be given such special treatment, approached with such reverent solemnity, enshrined in such an atmosphere of mystery? We handle the literature of our own language quite differently, perhaps because everyone is expected to learn to read and write that language before beginning to discover the great books of all time. (Incidentally, the general attitude toward music might be considerably changed if every child were taught to read and write notes in the same way and at the same age.)

Students of English and American literature are by no means limited to those who might in time become actors or public speakers or professional writers. They are introduced to the masterpieces of their language, and if this experience proves enjoyable, so much the better. It has little or nothing to do with mental discipline or drudgery of any kind.

While the phrase "music for fun" may be applied literally even to organized education, with no concession to entertainment as such, it has a far greater importance to human beings before and after the days of school and college. Children who treat music as a game are likely to develop their initial enthusiasm when the time arrives for more serious study. Conversely, many an adult will find real "fun" as both a listener and a participant in music of some sort, particularly when earlier opportunities have been neglected, perhaps because of bad teaching.

The fact should be squarely faced that only one out of many thousands of people can logically hope to attain any substantial skill in music, even as an amateur. But is there any reason for denying this enormous percentage of the comparatively untalented all opportunity for musical self-expression? Almost anyone can learn to make a few pleasant sounds on an autoharp, a harmonica, a guitar or ukulele, perhaps an accordion or even a piano. This is literally "music for fun," and from such modest performers must be recruited the audiences to make the work of our great artists worth while.

Gifts That Provide Music

It may come as a surprise to some parents that there are many gifts for children that have no connection with war, violence in general, or even outer space. Some of them might actually be related to music.

There are musical toys of many kinds that appeal to the very young, starting with the various rattles inevitably associated with babyhood. For children who have reached the crawling stage there are Mother Goose and Disney characters to be pushed or pulled around the floor, meanwhile giving out a rhythmic pattern of at least a few notes.

Some form of drum is likely to be discovered by almost any child at a tender age, for the noise-making instinct starts quite early. It is possible to control this throwback to savagery by selecting percussive toys of limited volume, like the smaller forms of the bongo family. But better yet is the suggestion of bells of various kinds, preferably tuned to definite pitches, like the keys of a xylophone. Such metal pieces, set on frames, are available in groups that vary from three tones up to the complete diatonic scale.

Of course there are music boxes of all sorts, which can introduce the permanent tunes of the world to children of any age, usually with the advantage of some colorful exterior. Even an artificial Christmas tree can be supplied with a musical base that plays "Silent Night" or some other melody of the season.

Children can begin to make a little music of their own much earlier than some parents realize. Toy trumpets, tin whistles and other primitive wind instruments are natural additions to the inevitable drums, and no great maturity is needed for an interest in tonettes, ocarinas ("sweet potatoes") and even recorders.

Actually the simplest wind instrument for producing immediate musical effects is the popular harmonica, or "mouth-organ." Both melody and harmony result automatically from the mere process of blowing in and drawing out the breath, and the newest methods of instruction simplify this approach through practical diagrams of familiar tunes, eliminating any need for notes.

Similarly the easiest of stringed instruments, known as the autoharp, makes any knowledge of notation quite unnecessary. This zither-like contraption is equipped with twelve keys, each producing a complete chord when held down over the strings, which are strummed with a pick or the fingers to produce any simple accompaniment to singing or whistling. An autoharp songbook needs only to have the letters representing the chords printed above the syllables on which they are to be played. Such an immediate performance is fascinating to adults as well as children.

In fact, there are plenty of musical gifts to fit every member of the family. Where talent and enthusiasm are present, the possible instruments range all the way from ukuleles and guitars to accordions, pianos and electronic organs. And for those without particular musical gifts or ambitions there are always phonographs, turntables and records. With the amazing developments of hi-fi and stereophonic sound, a new world has opened for music lovers, and there is now literally no limit to the possibilities of a musical Christmas or birthday.

Why Study Music?

THERE was a time when teachers of music, and particularly the piano, could think of only two reasons for such study: (1) to make money and (2) to "show off" to friends and become known as "the life of the party." Apparently it never occurred to these old-fashioned pedagogues that some adults (and perhaps children as well) might like to make a little music of their own just for their personal satisfaction, without any thought of either exhibitionism or commercialism.

Today there are more people than ever before with a sincere desire for musical self-expression, regardless of how limited their ability may be. So long as they themselves enjoy their playing, that is enough. From such modest amateurs must come a large part of the audience that alone can make the work of the professional artist worth while.

In dealing with adult beginners, the practical music teacher must realize that no special talent can be expected. There is no reason for using material beyond the grasp of the average child, for these mature pupils are basically in the same state of complete ignorance so far as music is concerned. They may be quite intelligent in other ways, and perhaps a more rapid progress may be expected because of their ability to concentrate and their determination to solve whatever problems they meet. But they cannot skip the fundamental steps and jump right into a style of music that might be considered suitable for their age. Simple pieces and simplifications of technique are just as necessary for the average adult as for the average child, regardless of any "great expectations" for the future.

Progressive educators now realize that the snobbery of the past was a serious mistake and kept millions from an honest enjoyment of music by making it a mystery and a matter of special privilege, talent and experience. "Music for Everybody" has become a literal possibility, from the standpoint of performance as well as listening, with more and more opportunities to play on an instrument of some sort for one's own pleasure, with no concern about any impressive skill or technique.

A big factor in this advance has been the development of the electronic organ, now available in a great number of practical models, often with two manuals and pedals, sometimes made still easier by a set of buttons (like an accordion's) controlling the essential chords, but always introducing the novice quickly and pleasantly to the black-and-white pattern common to all keyboard instruments.

Such "recreational instruments" as the harmonica, accordion, autoharp, guitar and ukulele have also proved helpful in encouraging the study of music by both adults and children. From such unpretentious beginnings, they can go on as far as they like in the practice and enjoyment of the greatest of all the arts. Meanwhile their musical activity can remain a sincere pleasure instead of becoming a drudgery or a duty or even a hypocritical pretense.

IV

THE POPULAR FIELD

In Defense of Popular Music

FOR some reason our music critics are still inclined to look upon popular music with contempt, making no effort to distinguish between the good and the bad materials in that field.

Eliminating the obvious trash aimed at illiterate sensation-seekers and concentrating on the lighter music of the world that has already proved its permanence, it becomes increasingly difficult to draw a definite line between the "popular" and the "serious" (absurdly called "classical" even when dealing with contemporary composition). The established masterpieces of operatic and symphonic literature generally contain at least a few passages that may frankly be labelled "popular," while the best of the lighter musical works, including folk songs and their imitations by Stephen Foster and others, have every right to the title of "classics" on the basis of their permanence.

Incidentally, why should a folk song of unknown authorship, with a rural or peasant background, be automatically considered superior to the same type of lyrics and music written by recognized members of the popular school, in urban surroundings? There are bad folk songs as well as bad products of Tin Pan Alley (not to speak of bad musical shows, grand operas and symphonies) and the good things achieve permanence through the established law of "the survival of the fittest."

A few direct comparisons will inevitably add to the difficulty of distinguishing between "popular" and "serious" (or "classical"!) music in general. Unquestionably the most popular tune in all grand opera is the Wedding March from Wagner's *Lohengrin*. But is this essentially any greater music than the best of Sousa's marches, for example? Is its popularity not largely due to habit and tradition? Are the unbalanced measures of the melody we know as "America" (also "God Save the Queen," "Heil dir im Siegerkranz," etc.) actually superior to Irving Berlin's definitely singable "God Bless America"? Could not the same composer's setting of the words on the Statue of Liberty be fairly called "serious music"?

Is the Brahms "Academic Festival Overture," based on German student songs, "popular" or "classical"? (One of the tunes is known to most of the world as "The Farmer in the Dell.") Can the Rodgers-Hammerstein "If I Loved You," which sounds like Brahms, be properly compared with that composer's own melodic inspirations? What about the "Soliloquy," and the instrumental waltzes in the same musical, *Carousel?* How should one appraise a song like the Kern-Hammerstein "All the Things You Are," or the same team's "Old Man River," now generally classed with the world's great folk music?

What happens to categorical classification when we hear the opening theme of a Mozart piano sonata as "In an 18th Century Drawing Room" or Flotow's "M'Appari" as "Marta" or the Largo from Dvorak's *New World Symphony* as "Goin' Home?" Can Verdi be accused of writing "popular" music in such numbers as "La Donna e Mobile" or the "Anvil Chorus" (successfully parodied by Sir Arthur Sullivan in *The Pirates of Penzance* and eventually emerging as "Hail, Hail, the Gang's All Here")?

Beethoven wrote gigantic symphonies, but among his most popular pieces are a little Minuet in G, a "Turkish March" and some country dances. (The finale of his *Violin Concerto* is a Russian folk song and there are Irish folk materials in his *Seventh Symphony*.) Schubert, Chopin and Tchaikovsky have all provided hit songs for Tin Pan Alley, with the last-named now credited with no less than seventeen popular arrangements of the beginning of his *Piano Concerto* alone. The list of such double lives is practically endless. Why not erase the dividing line altogether and let the test of time decide the issue?

Regarding Ragtime

ONE hears a great deal about ragtime nowadays, and there have been several attempts to put this form of popular music on television, with varying success. However, the term still seems to be widely misunderstood and there is room for considerable research on the part of those who write about ragtime or try to sing or play it or dramatize it on our home screens.

Actually the word means exactly what it implies: the tearing of a tune into tatters. This is accomplished by the simple device known to musicians as syncopation, which is nothing more than giving artificial accents to what would otherwise be unaccented notes. The fascination of ragtime lies in the fact that while the basic beat continues steadily, the rhythmic pattern of the melody continually anticipates or delays the natural accent, creating a definitely "ragged" effect.

There is a mistaken idea that the entire period preceding modern jazz (roughly covering the early years of the present century) can be classified as a ragtime era. Actually only the strongly syncopated music of that period can properly be called ragtime. Sentimental ballads and barbershop harmony have nothing whatever to do with the case unless they exhibit syncopation of some sort.

Equally mistaken is the belief that a national ragtime craze began with the appearance of Irving Berlin's popular song, "Alexander's Ragtime Band," in 1911. This was an excellent march tune, imitating the "ta-ra-ta-ra" of a trumpet and actual bugle calls, but its chorus contained only one small example of syncopation, and this was supplied by Stephen Foster in the line "And if you want to hear the 'Swanee River' played in ragtime." (The last two syllables are a practical example of simple syncopation, the first having a normal and the second an artificial accent.)

Mr. Berlin himself had written some real ragtime in his earlier "Yiddle on your Fiddle" and "Ragtime Violin," as well as the syncopated version of Mendelssohn's "Spring Song" as "That Mesmerizing Mendelssohn Tune." In 1911 he also produced "That Mysterious Rag," and his most concentrated syncopation appears in the later "Pack Up Your Sins," which literally tore its innocent tune to pieces.

But the technique of American ragtime was developed long before the present century, and its origins can actually be traced to the jungle drums themselves. Ben Harney is generally credited with being the first man to put down ragtime effects in notes for the piano. In 1897, the Witmarks published his *Ragtime Instructor,* in which he made it clear that ragtime was not a *kind* of music, but *a way of playing,* which could be applied to any composition by merely syncopating the melody.

Before that, Barney Fagan had written the raggy "My Gal Is a High Born Lady" and May Irwin's famous hit, "The New Bully," came even earlier. In fact there is real ragtime in so ancient a song as Dan Emmett's "Old Dan Tucker." An examination of the Negro spirituals reveals a free and frequent use of syncopation, especially in such lively tunes as "Little David, Play on Your Harp," "Heaven," etc.

The great classics of the past use this common method of shifting accents artificially, and folk music in general is full of syncopation. A good example of the latter is the Hungarian folk tune "The Heron," which Franz Liszt borrowed for his "Hungarian Fantasy." Beethoven's third "Leonore Overture" shows decided syncopation in its main theme, and those who argue that ragtime has no place in religious music should listen to the opening of Handel's "Hallelujah Chorus." (It is no longer a secret that those four syncopated notes supplied the start of the familiar "Yes, We Have No Bananas.")

Scott Joplin's "Maple Leaf Rag," dated 1899, is generally considered the popular classic of syncopation, but the same year brought forth another good example in "Smoky Mokes," and the syncopated cakewalk, "At a Georgia Camp Meeting," originated even earlier. Other titles could easily run into the thousands. The only trouble with ragtime today is that hardly anybody knows how to play or sing it.

Musical Embellishments

THERE is a curious and rather disturbing technique common in much of the popular piano-playing of today. It is the decoration of every note of melody by elaborate embellishments, usually arpeggios or fast scale passages.

There is nothing really new about this deliberate distortion of melody. For centuries the so-called musicians (and often the real ones as well) have been maltreating simple tunes in the same way. These frills and diddles and doodads have been characteristic of a great deal of the world's folk music and of some fairly serious compositions as well.

The Spanish flamenco style is a good example, as is also, in a simpler and more obvious form, the Swiss yodel. In both cases the singers "break" their voices and indulge in variations, apparently improvised on the spot, but actually representing a carefully studied technique. Jewish ritual music is of the same type, and a successful cantor must command a flexibility of voice amounting to that of a coloratura soprano.

Instrumental folk music is full of similar effects, as executed by the Hungarian cymbalom, the Russian balalaika and even the Spanish guitar, when played by an expert. Franz Liszt applied fancy treatments to many of the gypsy folk tunes of his native Hungary in a series of Rhapsodies which sometimes have more technique than substance, and are therefore adored by virtuoso concert pianists.

Unfortunately, Liszt applied a similar formula to the melodies of Schubert, Verdi and other composers, turning them into an exhibitionist's holiday. Chopin is reported to have told Liszt to keep his hands off his musical themes, even though Chopin himself was quite willing to indulge in occasional flights of melodic decoration.

The story is also told of Mendelssohn's accompaniment of a violinist in the Bach "Chaconne" (written for violin alone), evoking a rapturous review from no less a critic than Robert Schumann, who wrote that the great Leipzig master would surely have approved of this arrangement of his immortal composition!

With such examples in the interpretation of the classics, our popular pianists can hardly be blamed for dressing up everything they play with what to them is probably the last word in keyboard technique. While a conscientious concert artist is generally dedicated to playing a composition exactly as its creator intended it to be played, the popular musician often concentrates on getting away as far as possible from the original music and burying the melody in a cloud of overweighted embroidery.

Actually, there are still pianists, both popular and jazz, who show considerable originality and invention in their treatment of the often banal tunes of the Hit Parade. The danger is that those who think only in terms of digital dexterity will permanently influence the amateurs to believe that playing the piano is worth while only if one develops a spectacular technique with which to impress one's listeners.

Popular Songwriters

In general, our American public remembers its popular songs but not the men who wrote them. A few names stand out in each generation, like those of Richard Rodgers, Cole Porter and Irving Berlin today and George Gershwin, Jerome Kern and Victor Herbert in the past, with Stephen Foster as the real pioneer in the field.

Some enthusiasts may associate such hit-writers as Frank Loesser, Harold Rome, Bob Merrill, Frederick Loewe, Burton Lane, Arthur Schwartz and Rudolf Friml with their successful tunes, perhaps adding Sigmund Romberg, Vincent Youmans and others in the earlier years of this century.

But who wrote "Rudolph, the Red-Nosed Reindeer," "Love Letters in the Sand," "Buttons and Bows," "Diamonds Are a Girl's Best Friend," "Nature Boy," and that all-time pinnacle of nonsense, "Yes, We Have No Bananas"?

There is a strange custom, observed particularly in

radio and television, of naming only the interpreter of a popular song, never the composer and least of all the writer of the lyrics. To the vast listening public our greatest musical hits have been created by Perry Como, Bing Crosby, Frank Sinatra and Dinah Shore.

It is a mistake to belittle the songs that have emerged from Tin Pan Alley's factory, particularly those that have passed the test of time and are known in the profession as "standards." They are the best possible index to the everyday life, the manners, customs and idiosyncrasies of every generation.

The maudlin waltzes of the so-called Gay Nineties (perhaps better labelled "Naive") were characteristic of their time, as were the dance numbers of a later date and all the varieties of jazz that came with disillusionment after the first World War. We may even have to admit that the absurdities of Rock 'n' Roll truly reflect the violence, illiteracy and sex obsession of the present generation.

George M. Cohan was more than a creator of popular songs, for he shone as a playwright, producer, actor, singer and dancer. In his greatest inspiration, "Over There," which he modestly described as "just a bugle call," he gave our armed forces a musical stimulus that led eventually to Cohan's receiving a well-deserved Congressional Medal. His statue belongs in the Times Square he knew so well.

It may be significant also that the first American musician enshrined in the Hall of Fame was Stephen Foster, a popular songwriter.

"Dixie"
and "The Battle Hymn"

THE centennial of the War between the States drew considerable attention to the songs that were popular with the opposing forces in that gigantic struggle. While historians have been meticulous as to other details of the conflict, its musical significance has often been misrepresented, with many obvious contradictions and apparently wild guesses.

The two most important songs of the war unquestionably were "Dixie's Land" (generally abbreviated to "Dixie"), the musical battle cry of the South, and "The Battle Hymn of the Republic," which served the same purpose for the North. Ironically enough, the music and lyrics of the perennially popular "Dixie" were created by a Northerner, the minstrel Daniel Decatur Emmett of Ohio, while the melody of "The Battle Hymn" can be traced back to a camp-meeting song, "Say, Brothers, Will

You Meet Us?" composed by a Southerner named William Steffe.

Beyond these authentic and well-established facts, there is a wealth of violent disagreement concerning both songs. The truth about "Dixie" seems to be that "Old Dan" Emmett wrote the song in a New York boarding-house on a rainy Sunday in November, 1859, as a "walk-around" for Bryant's Minstrels, of which he was then a member. It had nothing whatever to do with war of any kind and was quite devoid of martial spirit, except for the fact that its lively tune is excellent for marching.

Apparently the first Southern performance of "Dixie" was at the Variety Theater in New Orleans, where Carlo Patti introduced it as a march of the Zouaves in the play *Pocahontas,* with Susan Denin singing the words. It was first published by Philip Werlein (whose store is still the musical center of New Orleans), giving no credit to Emmett, and then pirated repeatedly in the same anonymous fashion until Firth, Pond & Co. bought the copyright for three hundred dollars and brought it out with proper recognition of its true authorship. (Emmett himself claimed that this was his total income from the song.)

The title of "Dixie" had nothing to do with Mason's and Dixon's line, and was apparently given its Southern reference only after the appearance of Emmett's song. Its origin has been explained as the slang term for a ten dollar bill, known in New Orleans as a "Dixie" from the French word *dix*. There is also a story that "Dixie's Land" actually refers to a farm on Staten Island, whose owner was kind to his slaves. (This is contradicted by the reference to the "land of cotton.") According to Dan Emmett, the phrase "I wish I was in Dixie" was a common expression of nostalgia among show people.

"The Battle Hymn of the Republic" has also had its full share of controversy. The origin of the music is unquestioned, dating back to about 1856 and generally known as "Glory Hallelujah" or "The Hallelujah Song." It became popular as "John Brown's Body," but there is some doubt whether it actually referred to the abolitionist of Harper's Ferry. The words were first sung by the glee club of the "Tigers," a battalion of the Massachusetts Infantry stationed at Fort Warren, in Boston Harbor, and it has been claimed that they were intended as a joke on one of the soldiers whose name was John Brown. In any case, it was the Twelfth Massachusetts Regiment that spread the song all over the East on its way to the front. (There were other parodies also, including one which referred to Jefferson Davis.)

Concerning the authorship of the great words beginning "Mine eyes have seen the glory of the coming of the Lord" there is no argument. They were written by Julia Ward Howe after she heard the John Brown version sung by marching soldiers in Washington, D.C. The Reverend James Freeman Clarke is given credit for suggesting to her that the stirring music was worthy of a more dignified text. The story goes that the opening line came to her that night, while sleeping at the Willard Hotel. She lighted a candle, picked up a sheet of paper and completed the now famous poem before dawn.

Mrs. Howe, whose husband was Dr. Samuel Gridley Howe of Boston (they were introduced to each other by the poet Longfellow), sold her poem to *Atlantic Monthly* for ten dollars, and it appeared on the front page of the February issue of 1862. The rest is history.

Unwarlike War Songs

OUR national holidays bring inevitable reminders of the backgrounds of some of our patriotic music, as well as the songs that became popular during our wars of the past. What emerges most strikingly from a re-examination of such material is that comparatively few patriotic melodies were composed in honor of our country and that the songs most frequently associated with war actually had no military significance whatever.

"Yankee Doodle" originated as a joke played on our Colonial troops by a British officer, and the tune goes back to an English nursery rhyme about Lucy Locket who "lost her pocket." The melody of "The Star-Spangled Banner" originally fitted a rather ribald song about the Greek poet Anacreon, and was used for at least seventy-five different texts before it was officially accepted by President Hoover as our national anthem. Francis Scott Key's text was definitely patriotic, but referred to a single engagement in the War of 1812 and was first titled "The Defense of Fort McHenry."

A gay tune called "The President's March," written by Philip Phile of Philadelphia in honor of George Washington, was given the fine text of "Hail, Columbia, Happy Land" by Joseph Hopkinson, the son of Francis Hopkinson, a signer of the Declaration of Independence. But its words were later heard mostly in an obscene parody to the tune of "Ta-ra-ra-boom-de-ay."

The most popular song of the Spanish-American War was "A Hot Time in the Old Town Tonight," composed as an instrumental minstrel march by Theodore Metz, without the slightest reference to patriotism in the words later added by Joe Hayden. The first World War popularized "The Long, Long Trail" and "Tipperary," both written long before the outbreak of hostilities and without any thought of military significance. The one striking exception to the rule was George M. Cohan's "Over There," based on a bugle call and definitely inspired by the departure of our troops to Europe.

The Second World War required few popular songs, chiefly because marching was reduced to a minimum, and mechanical rather than human elements were emphasized. The "Beer Barrel Polka" is generally recognized as the song most popular among soldiers of all the Allied armies. (Noel Coward used it effectively in his British film, *In Which We Serve,* where a sailor plays the tune on a harmonica after his ship has been sunk.)

Irving Berlin's "God Bless America" was actually written in 1917 for a soldier show at Yaphank but considered too serious by its composer and kept hidden until Kate

Smith introduced it on Armistice Day, 1938. This is an almost unique example of words and music deliberately written to express patriotism and winning enormous popular success. (It has often been called our "unofficial national anthem" and many people prefer it to the more elaborate expressions of similar sentiments.) The fact remains that wars have seldom produced good music, or, for that matter, good art of any kind.

Political Campaign Songs

THE political campaign songs of the United States of America are practically endless. A number of them consisted merely of new words set to old tunes, and in general these were better than the completely original compositions. Fully ninety per cent of the total can be dismissed as atrocious.

"Tippecanoe and Tyler Too" must be considered one of the most famous campaign songs in our history, with music based on an earlier tune called "Little Pigs" and words by Alexander C. Ross. The nickname of "Tippecanoe" had been given to General William Henry Harrison as a result of his victory over the Indians in that battle, in 1811. President Harrison died only a month after his election, to be succeeded by his vice-president, John Tyler. There were several other "Tippecanoe" songs, plus an instrumental march and a quickstep.

One of our earliest campaign songs was called "Adams and Liberty," written for John Adams by Robert Treat

Paine in 1798 to the same British melody ("To Anacreon in Heaven") later used by Francis Scott Key for "The Star-Spangled Banner."

It is interesting to note some of the tunes that have been adapted for presidential campaign songs in the past. One of the most popular was the now almost forgotten "Old Rosin, the Beau," whose original version, possibly of Scotch descent, dates back to 1838. It was used for one of the "Tippecanoe" songs of 1840 and again, in 1844, the Whigs fitted its lilting 6-8 rhythm to two lyrics celebrating the virtues of Henry Clay, who was defeated by James K. Polk ("Old Hal of the West" and "The Mill-Boy of the Slashes"). Sixteen years later, a certain F. A. Simpkins wrote "Lincoln and Liberty" to the same tune, and finally, in 1872, some independents of the losing party produced a song called "Straight-out Democrat," and the music was still that of "Old Rosin, the Beau."

The rather ribald "Champagne Charlie" served as campaign material both for the defeated Horace Greeley and for the victorious Ulysses S. Grant. It is something of a surprise to find the German student song, "Crambambuli" (referring to a popular brand of wine) slowed up for the hymn-like "Come, Gallant Whigs" of 1848. The familiar "Marines' Hymn," a favorite of New York's late Mayor La Guardia, also pops up unexpectedly in praise of the unsuccessful team of Blaine and Logan, who also turned George Root's "Tramp, tramp, tramp, the boys are marching" into "Hark, hark, hark the chorus swelling."

One of the many versions of what most people call "The Old Gray Mare" had words to the effect that "Old

Abe Lincoln Came Out of the Wilderness." (It may be remembered by some disappointed radio listeners that the program "Stop the Music" called it "Come Out of the Wilderness".) The Great Emancipator was also represented by "Yankee Doodle Lincoln" and several other songs. More recently we have had "Wilson, That's All," including a phrase from "Tammany," "Coolidge, Our President," a very dull song, and an "F.D.R. Grand March" which quoted from "Hail to the Chief" but could not compete with "Happy Days Are Here Again." Composers should really be warned against writing political campaign songs.

Irish Songs

SOME of the songs of Ireland may have had an English musical origin. "My Lodging is on the Cold Ground," while used by Tom Moore for his famous words, "Believe Me If All Those Endearing Young Charms," seems definitely English rather than Irish and has been attributed to Matthew Lock. It is perhaps best known today as "Fair Harvard."

Cornell's familiar Alma Mater song, "Far Above Cayuga's Waters," also known as "Amici," used the tune of the Irish song "Annie Lisle." It has been appropriated by many other colleges and schools all over America.

One of Ireland's finest melodies is the so-called "Londonderry Air," or "Irish Tune from County Derry." It has inspired the lyrics "Would God I Were the Tender Apple Blossom," by Katharine Tynan Hinkson, and also "Danny Boy," by Fred E. Weatherly. Percy Grainger made a choral arrangement of it, substituting vocal syllables for words, and Fritz Kreisler's violin transcription is well known. He used the title "Farewell to Cucullain," which may have been applied to an early version of the same tune.

Thomas Moore is often credited with composing the music of his Irish songs, but probably did no more than edit traditional melodies to fit his words. Charles Villiers Stanford, in his Preface to Moore's *Irish Melodies,* says: "There is scarcely a melody which Moore has left un-altered, and, as a consequence, unspoilt." Yet Moore's versions have become the popular ones, and it is through him that Irish music is best known.

Moore's words, "The Harp that Once thro' Tara's Halls," are set to an old tune called "Gramachree." Tara Castle was the traditional location of the Irish harpers' contests, which originally inspired the Minnesingers of the Wartburg. "Has Sorrow Thy Young Days Shaded?" goes back to a tune called "Sly Patrick." "The Last Rose of Summer," immortalized in Flotow's *Martha,* is a combination of Moore's lyrics and an old melody called "The Groves of Blarney." The music of "The Minstrel Boy," one of Moore's finest songs, is originally "The Moreen," whose title is the diminutive of Mor or Moira, a girl's name.

Samuel Lover, who wrote "The Low-backed Car," "Barney O'Hea," and other popular Irish songs, and who was a composer as well as a poet, will be remembered also as the grandfather of that genial Irish-American musician, Victor Herbert.

"The Little Red Lark," with words revised by Alfred Perceval Graves, was originally "The Little Red Lark of the Mountain." "The Little Stalk of Barley" supplied

Francis A. Fahy with the tune for "Little Mary Cassidy." Edward de Vere wrote the words of "The Snowy-breasted Pearl," adapting the idea and melody of an old song, "Pearl of the White Breast."

The rousing tune of "St. Patrick's Day" has long been considered unofficially as Ireland's national air, and goes back to the first decade of the eighteenth century. It was played by the Irish war-pipers at the Battle of Fontenoy in 1745, and was first printed in Rutherford's *Country Dances* in 1749. Isaac Bickerstaffe, in 1762, set one of his songs in *Love in a Village* to this tune, and Tom Moore, in 1810, turned it into "Tho' Dark Are Our Sorrows." Its rhythmic pattern is similar to that of the familiar "Irish Washerwoman."

Beethoven arranged many of the Irish tunes, including the historic "Garry Owen," to which he gave three different interpretations, but his materials were not all authentic. It has been claimed that Beethoven's *Seventh Symphony* was strongly influenced by Irish music, and that its Finale theme is an Irish folk tune.

"The Wearing of the Green," which has caused its full share of political and private brawls, was an Irish street-ballad of 1798. It was altered by Dion Boucicault, who added a third stanza, referring to America as a haven for those who suffered from tyranny. The name of Bonaparte was often substituted for that of Napper Tandy in the song. "Killarney" was written by Michael William Balfe, who also composed the popular opera, *The Bohemian Girl*.

One more Irish song deserves mention here because it has served widely as a basis for parodies and topical verses, for which purpose it has a tune that is just about ideal. This song is "The Son of a Gambolier." It was best known at one time through a set of verses in German dialect called *Dunderbeck*. American colleges know it chiefly as "A Rambling Wreck from Georgia Tech."

Where and how it originated no one seems to know. But it has certainly been sung for a long, long time, and with countless different sentiments. It is the father of many of the tunes in 6-8 time which provide that simplest of rhythmic patterns and lead to equally simple rhyme schemes, tempting the amateur poets of all the world to write their own words and hear them sung with hearty enthusiasm. This is Ireland's real contribution to popular music.

Credit for Popular Hits

In the field of popular music the composer definitely takes a back seat. An arranger may be of greater significance in the making of a song hit, but the public is generally aware only of the singer or ensemble or band leader most consistently associated with the performance of the number.

This attitude is encouraged by disk jockeys and masters of ceremonies, who seldom mention the name of a popular composer but always play up the performers, whether on records or in "live" appearances. Many a listener actually receives the impression that a popular hit was created by the singer or group immediately responsible for its interpretation.

Such a psychology easily communicates itself to the stars of the entertainment world, who never hesitate to distort the materials given them even by outstanding creative talents. It is frequently painful to hear the liberties taken with the melodies of a Gershwin, a Kern, a Cole

Porter or a Richard Rodgers. Apparently the "song stylists" are utterly unaware of the virtues which made such composers successful. They ignore a well-made melodic line, change the rhythm to suit their whims (or those of an arranger) and sometimes even alter the words. There seems to be an unwritten law among popular singers that one must never come down squarely on the beat, but always anticipate or delay the accent slightly, so as to destroy whatever continuity the song may originally have had.

Strangely enough, this insulting treatment has occasionally given a new life to an old-time hit or "standard" which would probably have failed to achieve its original popularity if it had been interpreted in the current style. Unquestionably the interpreter outshines the composer of America's popular music today.

In the field of serious composition the situation is quite different. Here the highest compliment that can be paid a performer is to say that the intentions of the composer were meticulously carried out. It has been a mark of distinction for such conductors as Toscanini, Bruno Walter, Fritz Reiner and Pierre Monteux.

Yet even serious musicians often find it hard to resist the temptation of tampering with the notes they are given to play or sing, perhaps also ignoring a composer's specific directions for the interpretation of a composition. Singers are perhaps more culpable than the instrumentalists in this respect. The tenor has yet to be found who will consent to delivering the final high note of "Celeste Aida" *pianissimo,* as Verdi instructed in his opera *Aida.*

Orchestral conductors find it hard to escape the urge

to imprint their individual personalities on every piece of music they interpret. After all, there is the ever present danger of being called a mere "time-beater," and the music critics themselves go out of their way to find some touches of novelty in the reading of a familiar classic. Even when every tradition of tempo and dynamics is faithfully respected, a conductor can make his performance stand out visually by entering with physical exuberance into every detail of expression. Such gyrations are for the benefit of the audience, not the players, for these hard-working artisans have been thoroughly drilled in rehearsal and need no dramatic reminders of how each measure is to be performed.

"Payola" Is an Old Story

To anyone at all active in the business of popular music, "payola" is nothing new. It has been known (and deplored) for years, but little or nothing was done about it until quite recently.

To those who may think that "payola" is an Italian musical term or a station on the Main Line of the Pennsylvania Railroad, it should perhaps be explained that this now common word is merely Tin Pan Alley slang for bribery. Let it be admitted also that the popular music business could hardly exist without some system of financial favors and inducements. A dependence on merit alone is a practical impossibility in this strange and secretive industry.

First of all, the average music publisher is totally incapable of telling in advance just how successful a song may become, even if it is insistently brought to the attention of the public. But he is often ready to spend plenty of money to secure the necessary hearings which may, if he is lucky, produce a favorable reaction. Once the popularity of a song is established, the positions are reversed. Singers and band leaders then compete for the chance to perform and record it, make their own arrangements and enhance their reputations by individual interpretations.

The problem is to get past the introductory stage and persuade enough artists and middlemen to give a new composition a chance to prove its appeal to listeners. Since the merits and potentialities of such a song are an absolutely unknown quantity until it has passed this test, there is a natural temptation to reward in some way those who have been helpful in its promotion. Few business men have ever been known to say, in effect, "I want your good-will and co-operation, but don't expect any favors from me." In the field of popular music, such an attitude would be fatal.

So it all becomes largely a question of degree. Cash payments to disk jockeys and other influential individuals are obviously reprehensible, with equal guilt on the part of the givers and the takers. But there are subtler ways of showing appreciation for favors, past, present or future, and it may be doubted whether these basic forms of bribery can ever be completely eradicated.

The real sins against morality in the music business are two-fold: (1) the refusal to help even a worthy composition without payment in advance; (2) the willingness to promote obvious trash as long as the bribe is sufficiently large.

Currently, the outstanding proof of the evils of "payola" is in the emergence of the festering sore known as Rock 'n' Roll. This disgraceful form of musical illiteracy could never have fastened so firm a hold on our teen-agers without the constant influence of "payola" in the background. Those responsible for its promotion were fully aware of its abysmal worthlessness but willingly prostituted themselves for pay. As a result, the "hit parade" ceased to represent music actually enjoyed by the public as a whole. The listing of supposedly popular favorites has for some time been fundamentally dishonest.

Parallel Melodic Patterns

IF lawyers, judges and juries only realized how many musical compositions open with identical phrases, entirely by accident, there might be fewer plagiarism suits. For most of this litigation is based on only a few notes, representing often not even a parallel melodic sequence.

Leonard Bernstein recently pointed out a number of serious pieces beginning with the four opening notes of "How Dry I Am." This writer has made a list of 256 similar uses of this short phrase. Yet every composition is actually different and individual, merely using the same starting-point as a springboard.

When Dimitri Tiomkin's "The High and the Mighty" was attacked by an optimistic plaintiff, it was not difficult to find parallels to his first four notes, such as the familiar opening of Tchaikovsky's popular *Piano Concerto,* the "Playhouse 90" theme and "The Sidewalks of New York." All six notes of the phrase in question occurred in a Mahler symphony and an old pop tune, and actually there was only one note shared by both plaintiff and defendant. The former could easily have been accused of borrowing his tune from Fritz Kreisler's "Liebesfreud," which contains the identical six tones of his opening melodic phrase in the same order.

There is a sequence of eight tones which occurs at the start of at least half a dozen absolutely different compositions, entirely by coincidence. One of them is the "Habanera" from Bizet's *Carmen;* another is the Chaminade piece called "Autumn" with an exact parallel in one of the "Sea Pieces" of MacDowell; the sequence turns up again in both "Andalusia" and "The Breeze and I," with only a rhythmic difference in Victor Herbert's "Beatrice Barefacts."

The ancient five-tone scale, represented by the pattern of the black keys on the piano, may be found at the start of the old "Stumbling" tune by Zez Confrey, Friml's "Allah's Holiday," Irving Berlin's "Always" and Hoagy Carmichael's "Old Buttermilk Sky," not to speak of its obvious appearance in the *Scotch Symphony* of Mendelssohn.

Georges Auric's hit, "Song of the Moulin Rouge," claimed as plagiarism by a Washington amateur and resulting in a hung jury, could far more easily have been compared with at least a dozen common bugle calls, and actually appears on the familiar dining-room chime, as well as in *Hansel and Gretel* and elsewhere. "Buttons and Bows" was successfully defended against an absurd claim of infringement by direct comparison with several folk tunes, including the familiar nursery rhyme "I love coffee, I love tea."

When one thinks of the number of times that almost identical bridge hands appear by mere chance in dealing a pack of fifty-two cards, the almost automatic duplication of short musical phrases, all based on a scale of only seven different tones, is hardly surprising. Viewed in the light of this very short arm of coincidence, the great majority of claims against the musical creations of reputable composers must be dismissed as pure nonsense.

It has been clearly proved that it is very dangerous to let a musically ignorant jury decide whether one tune has or has not been copied from another. The law in such cases demands not only a striking similarity or even identity, covering a substantial portion of both compositions, but a clear proof of access to or contact with the plaintiff's work on the part of the defendant. Similarity as such cannot be considered reliable evidence of copying.

If a song is so well known as to imply an almost universal familiarity, the "access" may be taken for granted, and a striking similarity may be considered at least unconscious plagiarism, for which a defendant is just as liable as if deliberate copying had been proved. This was actually the case years ago, when Fred Fischer sued Jerome Kern on the charge of having taken the boogie bass of the popular "Dardanella" for his own "Kalua." The identity represented only a single measure of music, but it was repeated throughout both songs, thereby making it both essential and substantial, and could honestly be considered an outstanding and common characteristic. In view of Mr. Kern's recognized integrity and the obviously unintentional plagiarism, he was assessed with only minimum damages by a fair-minded judge.

The same verdict was pronounced against Joseph Sant-
ley's "There's Yes, Yes in Your Eyes," although in this
case the token damages resulted from a clever plea by the
defendant's counsel, Nathan Burkan, who argued that the
plaintiff's song had no commercial success, whereas Sant-
ley's hit was due largely to efficient merchandising of
material whose basic value had not been proved. These
two historic litigations were almost unique in the fundamental justification of their claims, and in both cases a
referee or group of adjudicators might have arrived at an
equally fair decision.

Certainly such intermediaries would not have permitted the horrible miscarriage of justice that occurred in
the case of a song called "Starlight," which clearly shared
a common ancestor with the plaintiff's totally unknown
composition, without the slightest proof of access or contact, but was nevertheless branded as plagiarism by a con-
fessedly ignorant judge.

This whole problem of musical plagiarism comes down
to a few simple questions which our judges, our juries
and our lawyers too often fail to grasp: Is the similarity
so striking and substantial as to justify the suspicion of
copying? Was the defendant completely dependent on this
one possible source for his melody? Is there positive proof
of his familiarity with the plaintiff's tune? And finally,
from the standpoint of ordinary common sense, is there
any reason to believe that a reputable composer would
deliberately steal the property of a comparative novice in
the commercial field of popular music?

America's Great Musicals

IF this be heresy, make the most of it: the best of our modern Broadway musical shows are the greatest not only of our time but of all time.

The world has never before known light stage music like that of Jerome Kern's *Show Boat,* the masterpieces of Rodgers and Hammerstein, Cole Porter's *Kiss Me, Kate,* or Leonard Bernstein's *West Side Story,* to name only a few of the more obvious examples. These musical comedies or operettas or plays with music or whatever you wish to call them are infinitely superior to the imitations of European models created by Victor Herbert, Sigmund Romberg, Rudolf Friml and other composers of the past. It may be argued that they surpass even the best of Franz Léhar, Offenbach and Johann Strauss.

All of these men wrote beautiful melodies, but the books of their shows were generally poor and therefore cannot, as a rule, lend themselves to successful revivals today. The plots were almost uniformly maudlin, telling and re-telling the same old story of two lovers temporarily separated by impossible misunderstandings and reunited in the last act, with interludes by a dialect comedian and songs thrown in on cue without any relation to the story or the characters. The action usually took place in a completely imaginary country with an absurd name, permitting the use of fancy costumes and uniforms but having not the faintest connection with reality of any kind.

Did anyone ever really identify with the fate of the hero or heroine in any of those musicals? Was any problem of importance solved or even suggested? Did the artificial quarrels and contrived obstacles make any sense whatever? Granted that the tunes were generally good and that the songs are still sung and will continue to be sung indefinitely, is there a single story in this light-operatic repertoire of the past worth remembering today?

Perhaps the greatest superiority of the modern American musicals lies in the fact that so many of them are based upon books of distinction. When Kern and Oscar Hammerstein II pioneered in musical realism with their epoch-making *Show Boat,* they built upon the foundation of an excellent novel by Edna Ferber. Richard Rodgers and Lorenz Hart based *Pal Joey* on a series of brilliant stories by John O'Hara. Later, with Hammerstein as a partner, Rodgers created what may in time be remembered as the three outstanding light scores of all time: *Carousel,* adapted from Molnar's *Liliom, South Pacific,* from the tales of James Michener, and *The King and I,* from the almost unique biographical record of Anna Lenowens.

To these obvious examples of important subject matter one might add the observation that both *Kiss Me, Kate* and *West Side Story* owe their plots to Shakespeare, the first to the comic *Taming of the Shrew* and the second to the tragic *Romeo and Juliet.* Nor should it be overlooked that the success of *My Fair Lady* is largely due to the biting wit of George Bernard Shaw's *Pygmalion.*

Actual history has been presented on the musical comedy stage in such works as *The Sound of Music,* dealing with the adventures of the Trapp Family, *Fiorello,* obviously examining the career of New York's Mayor La Guardia, and *Gypsy,* in which Ethel Merman brought to life the fabulous mother of the equally unusual sisters, Gypsy Rose Lee and June Havoc. In this category belong also Irving Berlin's *Annie, Get Your Gun* and *Call Me Madam,* the former concentrating on the marksmanship of Annie Oakley and the showmanship of Buffalo Bill, while the latter lightly spoofed the political and social activities of ambassadress Perle Mesta.

These are all good stories, founded either on actual fact or on convincing fiction of the highest order. Their musical settings are not confined to a mere succession of good songs strung upon a superficial suggestion of plot. Every musical number is intimately related to the action or to the development of character and personality. There are no songs thrown in just for their own sake.

George Gershwin's Pulitzer Prize-winning political satire, *Of Thee I Sing,* should probably be included among the great musical shows of our time. *Porgy and Bess,* for which the Heywards' drama of Negro life provided a solid background, actually belongs in the category of opera rather than musical comedy. Close to the same standard is

Frank Loesser's *The Most Happy Fella,* successfully based upon Sidney Howard's play, *They Knew What They Wanted.* The same composer's *Guys and Dolls* made good use of Damon Runyon's incredible New York characters.

The most surprising popular success on our contemporary musical stage has been that of *West Side Story,* created by such talents as Leonard Bernstein, Arthur Laurents, Stephen Sondheim and Jerome Robbins. The music is largely written in a complicated modern idiom, although there are also several highly singable melodies. That *West Side Story* should be a box office hit as well as an artistic success (including the film version) is a clear indication that the new standards for Broadway musicals have become firmly established. There is no longer a place for the conventional song-and-dance show. The American stage can hold its head high when comparing its best musical efforts with those of the past; and the importance of music is by no means limited to the classic masterpieces of the most serious composers.

INDEX

N

O

Oakley, Annie, 208

Oboe, 74

Ocarina, 163

Offenbach, Jacques, 114, 206
(*La Perichole*, 114)

O'Hara, John, 207
(*Pal Joey*, 207)

Old Abe Lincoln, 190

Old Grey Mare, The, 190

Old Hal o' the West, 190

Old Rosin the Beau, 190

Olive Mead Quartet, 42

Opera, 6, 7, 9, 11, 16, 20, 45-7, 73, 88, 90, 94, 97-8 113-4, 126, 137, 172

Oratorio, 7, 9, 11

Orchestra, 16, 21, 73, 74-6, 149, 152, 159

Organ, 164, 166

P

Paderewski, I. J., 64, 153
(*Minuet*, 153)

Paine, Robert Treat, 152, 189-90
(*Adams and Liberty*, 152, 189)

Paine, Thomas, 152

Palestrina, G. P., 109-10
(*The Strife Is O'er*, 109-10)

Patti, Adelina, 28

Patti, Carlo, 183

Percussion, 111-2, 162

Peterborough Colony, 64

Peter Pan, 62

Petrillo, J. C., 158

Phile, Philip, 151
(*President's March*, 151, 187)

Philipp, Isidor, 63

Phonograph, 82, 154-5

Pianists, 30, 177-9

Piano Music, 9, 11, 25, 77, 177

Picasso, 61
(*Three Musicians*, 61)

Pierrot, 61

Polish Music, 38

Polk, James K., 190

Polonaise, 38

Popular Songs, 12, 13, 20, 22, 24, 34, 80-81, 90, 95, 99, 100, 102, 135-6, 171-3, 180-1, 196-7, 199-201, 202-5, 206-8

Porter, Cole, 22, 58, 99, 180, 196-7, 206, 208
(*Kiss Me, Kate*, 58, 59, 206, 208)

Potemkin, Count, 28

Program Music, 7-8, 15-16, 33

Prokofiev, Serge, 38

Prosody, 101-3, 113-4

Puccini, Giacomo, 89, 126
(*Tosca*, 126)

Purcell, Henry, 59
(*Come unto These Yellow Sands*, 59)

R

Rachmaninoff, Sergei, 19

Radio, 82, 89, 92, 100

Ragging the Scale, 117

Ragtime, 174-6

X

Y